# STOCKHOLM ECONOMIC STUDIES

Published by writers connected with the Institute for Social Sciences
of Stockholm University.

## No. 4.

# STUDIES OF
# DIFFERENTIAL FERTILITY
# IN SWEDEN

# STUDIES OF DIFFERENTIAL FERTILITY IN SWEDEN

BY

KARL ARVID EDIN

AND

EDWARD P. HUTCHINSON

LONDON

P. S. KING & SON, LTD.

ORCHARD HOUSE, 14 GREAT SMITH STREET
WESTMINSTER

The publication of this volume has
been aided by a grant from the
Längman Fund

*Printed in Stockholm 1935
Victor Pettersons Bokindustriaktiebolag*

# CONTENTS

## CHAPTER I

## CHAPTER II

## CHAPTER III

## CHAPTER IV

# LIST OF TABLES IN THE TEXT

# LIST OF APPENDIX TABLES.

# FOREWORD.

Karl Arvid Edin, Docent and Director of the Demographic Institute in the University of Stockholm and Department Chief in the Swedish Central Statistical Board, has, over a period of years, made a series of original and important investigations of differential fertility in Sweden. Although the major results of these investigations have not had wide circulation, since they have appeared only in Swedish, and were adressed only to a public technically informed as to the Swedish sources, certain fragmentary reports in English and German have aroused international interest among students in this field. In recognition of this interest, it has seemed advisable to make a more complete report for non-Swedish students, and to include a comprehensive and critical analysis of the Swedish sources, the materials and the sampling techniques used in certain of Docent Edin's investigations. To this end, the Institute for Social Sciences of the University of Stockholm arranged with the Social Science Research Council of New York to release Dr. Edward P. Hutchinson, of Harvard University, to collaborate in analyzing the data and in bringing out the present volume.

The material in this volume represents only a small part of Docent Edin's total contribution in this field, and this report should be regarded more as an introduction than as a complete survey.

Grateful acknowledgement is made to the City Council of Stockholm for financial support of this study and to the Längman Fund for a grant to aid its publication. Professor Dorothy Swaine Thomas of Yale University and the Institute for Social Sciences, Stockholm, has given valuable advice during the preparation of the manuscript.

Stockholm, June 1935.

*Gösta Bagge.*

# STUDIES OF
# DIFFERENTIAL FERTILITY
# IN SWEDEN

# STUDIES OF
# DIFFERENTIAL FERTILITY
# IN SWEDEN

## CHAPTER I.

## INTRODUCTION.

THE direction of development followed by demographic studies of human fertility has been towards progressively greater specificity of comparative analysis. The immediate products of this development have been, in the first place, more accurate techniques for measuring fertility, in the second place, classification of original material into more specific and homogeneous subdivisions. Whereas earlier investigations of fertility were generally made with reference to administrative units of population only, attention is now being directed particularly towards comparative study of the fertility rates obtaining within population groups, analysis being made not only by political divisions but also according to sociological factors such as education, occupation and economic status. This type of study which attempts to determine the differences in reproductivity, or »differential fertility»,[1] existing between the various social strata of a political unit of population at present constitutes one of the major branches of demographic investigation.

Studies of differential fertility have, to a considerable extent, directly adopted the original material and the statis-

[1] As used below the term »differential fertility» is applied only in connection with sociological subdivision of an administrative unit of population — that is, where classification is on a qualitative rather than on a purely geographical basis.

tical methods employed in the more general type of fertility investigation. With detailed analysis according to social status, however, additional demands for detail and accuracy are made upon the source material, and a reexamination of the measures of fertility to be employed becomes necessary to verify their continued applicability. In the series of investigations of differential fertility in Sweden reported below, the statistical data and methods were expressly chosen to detect social differentials in fertility. The primary emphasis in these investigations was on the quality of the original data; the methodological keynote throughout was the discovery of the fertility differentials by means of accuracy and refinement of material rather than by dependence on elaboration of statistical technique alone. Similarly, in interpretation of the data, the criterion of consistency was employed uniformly in preference to statistical measures of significance.

The procedure described below being intimately associated with, really a product of, the Swedish statistical system, a brief outline of the pertinent features of this organization is given by way of introduction, followed by a discussion of the types of material and statistical measures of fertility to be employed.

## A. Swedish Statistical Organization.[1]

The Swedish political unit is the community, usually coinciding with the corresponding unit of the state church organization, the parish (församling). Responsibility for the registration of births, deaths and marriages has, since 1686,

[1] For the explicit directions concerning the keeping of the Swedish parish registers see A. Lysander and G. Forkman, »Kyrkobokföringen», Svenska Kyrkans Diakonistyrelses Bokförlag, Stockholm, 1929. For a more general account see League of Nations, Statistical Organization: Statistical Handbook Series, No. 6, »The Official Vital Statistics of the Scandinavian Countries and the Baltic Republics», Geneva, 1926. For an account of the history and development of the Swedish statistical organization see E. Arosenius, »Bidrag till det Svenska Tabellverkets Historia», Kungliga Boktryckeriet, Stockholm, 1928; or »The History and Organization of Swedish Official Statistics», The History of Statistics, edited by John Koren, New York, 1918.

been placed on the local clergy. The system has since 1750
been extended so that the parish registers now form the
basis of the Swedish official statistics. The registers kept
in each parish are: —

1. the parish book,
2. book of births and baptisms,
3. book of deaths and burials,
4. book of confirmations,
5. book of banns and marriages,
6. book of in-migrants,
7. book of out-migrants, and
8. book of »non-existent» (residence unknown).

Of these, the parish book (församlingsbok) is the central
register, containing a summary of all information included
in the other registers. In it are given the names of all inhabitants of the parish, grouped according to family and place
of residence. For each person is recorded date and place of
birth, marital and familial status, religion, occupation, date
of death of the deceased, date of beginning and end of
marriage (by death or divorce), date of in-migration and
place of previous residence of those moving into the parish,
date of removal and place of subsequent residence of out-
migrants, as well as notations concerning military service,
criminal record, physical and mental deficiency.

All persons moving into a community must bring with
them a migration certificate (flyttningsbetyg) from the
parish office of previous registration. This certificate is
essentially an abstract of the parish book record and is to
insure accuracy of information. An acknowledgment of
receipt of the migration certificate is sent back to the office
of issue to complete the record concerning place of location
of out-migrants.

For all official purposes a person is regarded as a resident
of the parish where registered. Deaths are thus reported as
of place of official residence regardless of actual place of
death, and births are similarly assigned to the parish in
which the parents are registered (for illegitimate children,

residence of mother). The accuracy of maternity hospital records is incidentally assured by the requirement that all expectant mothers be provided with an official abstract of their parish book record on admission to the hospital.

Place of official residence can be changed only by the taking out of a migration certificate and the presentation of it in another parish. The official population of the parish is the registered in contrast to the actual population, but the difference is comparatively slight, only about one-half of one percent of the total population living elsewhere than in place of registration at the time of the 1920 census.

The completeness of the parish book population register is assured by annual checking with the list of inhabitants obtained by the yearly household registration (mantalsskrivning). All persons missing for two consecutive years are transferred to the book of the »non-existent» to prevent inclusion in the population figures of inviduals having only a statistical existence. If subsequently located these »non-existent» are again registered.

Since 1860 the Swedish decennial census has been based not on direct enumeration of the population but on abstracts of the parish books, these abstracts prepared by the local parish offices and sent to the Royal Census Bureau. In the 1930 abstracts were given the names of all persons, grouped according to households, registered in the parish on the date of the census (December 31, 1930), together with status in family, marital status, year of marriage, occupation and status in occupation, year and place of birth, nationality, year of last movement into the community, community of previous residence, mental and physical defects. Note was also made of all persons living in villages of at least two hundred inhabitants.

This material was checked and supplemented at the Census Bureau by two independent sources of information: —

1. the 1930 household registration lists (Mantalslängd);
2. the income and property tax returns for 1930.

The former of these, a compulsory annual report for taxation purposes, provided a list of all persons present in each household and was made one and one-half months before the census. The latter was made one and one-half months after the census. These two sources gave not only information concerning income and property, education and incapacitation, but also completed and corrected the statements of occupation contained in the parish book abstracts. The latter check was desirable since the parish book record of occupation was usually made upon entrance to the community and therefore may have been made at a time considerably before the census. Report was also given of the total number of children born to each married couple, including children dying before the census data and children not living with parents. In the household registration forms for 1930 was included an additional question as to occupation and status within occupation in 1925.

The official birth statistics are similarly based on the parish registers, nominal abstracts of the births registers being sent each year to the Central Statistical Bureau.

The only exception to the organization outlined above is in the city of Stockholm where it was found necessary to institute a municipal Registration Bureau (Mantalskontoret). While not supplanting the parish office in registration of vital statistics, this bureau has taken over the function of civil population registration in Stockholm. The information available is essentially the same as that to be obtained from the various parish registers.

## B. Types of Statistical Material.

Aside from special statistics derived from genealogies, questionnaires, and so forth, the original material for the study of fertility rates is official in origin and of one of two types according as the nativity data are obtained by the continuous registration of vital statistics or by retrospective reporting. In the latter case, the data are typically obtained in connection with census enumerations where such information as year of birth of parents, year of marriage, total number and year of birth of living children is recorded for each family.

In general, both types of nativity material, the one based on continuous birth registration, the other on retrospective reporting, possess certain relative advantages but also certain inherent weaknesses if detailed classification is to be made with respect to social status. The principal difficulties encountered with birth registration material, aside from the deficiencies of information or the actual errors which may be found in any nativity data, are the following: —

(1) Reporting of births according to actual place of birth. This error, arising from failure to reassign all births to place of residence of parents, is unfortunately present in the vital statistics of most countries, increasing the computed birth rates of communities containing maternity hospitals while depressing the rates of adjacent areas, in particular invalidating direct comparison of urban and rural birth rates.[1]

(2) Lack of accurate population figures. Although the number of registered births may be reported annually, population figures are usually obtainable only at ten-year intervals, estimates given by interpolation or extrapolation becoming progressively less reliable as the interval of estimation and the detail of sociological classification increases.

(3) Lack of correspondence in classification of births and population. This difficulty, the greatest inherent in the registration type of material, is entirely apart from actual lack of information; it increases rapidly with the complexity of subdivision, and is particularly serious in connection with sociological classifications. Just as the geographical assignment of births may not correspond to that of the entire population (paragraph 1 above), so even if obtainable the classification of nativity data according to occupation of father, ancestry of parents, or economic status of family, for example, may not correspond to the divisions employed in census tabulations.

These sources of error are eliminated in the retrospective type of material: children are recorded according to place of

[1] For a discussion of the difficulties involved in comparison of urban and rural nativity and population figures see for example W. Winkler, Grundriss der Statistik, II, Gesellschaftsstatistik, Berlin, 1933. Pp. 57—58.

residence of parents, the population figures are automatically included together with the recorded number of births, and the correspondence in sociological classification of children and of parents is complete. In compensation, however, other disadvantages appear, in particular the following:

(1) Intrusion of a trend element. In the case of retrospective data the total absolute fertility from time of marriage to census date may be influenced by a trend factor not present in short time observations. While this may be an advantage if differential trends in fertility are to be studied, it further complicates statistical analysis. In the case of the longer marriage durations, coupled with possible changes in social status or even actual changes in the significance of arbitrary sociological classifications, this trend factor may greatly reduce the interpretability of observations.

(2) Possibility of selection. In as much as the only entire families included in retrospective material are those in which the parents have survived up to time of the census, there is at least theoretical possibility of selection, especially if only completed families are considered. It must be admitted, however, that there is no convincing evidence of association between longevity and fertility.[1]

(3) Change of residence or of social status of parents between marriage and census. Although selection or subdivision of material may eliminate dissimilarities with regard to age distribution of parents and duration of marriage in the subgroups compared, residence, occupation and social status at the time of census may differ considerably from those in the early and more fertile periods of the longer marriages. It has been shown that fertility is apparently affected by changes in economic status;[2] without further developing the point it is obvious that introduction of a possibility of change seriously impairs the significance of sociological classifications.

[1] See for example, Xarifa Sallume and Frank Notestein: »Trends in the Size of Families completed prior to 1910 in various social Classes», Am. J. Soc. XXXVIII, No. 3. P. 402, November, 1932.

[2] See Sydenstricker and Perrott: »Sickness, Unemployment, and Fertility», Milbank Memorial Fund Quarterly, Vol. 12, 1934; also chapter IV, section F, below.

These are the principal difficulties to be encountered in the use of official nativity data in the determination of social class differentials in fertility. In the series of investigations of fertility differentials in Sweden reported below they were eliminated in so far as possible, principally by careful selection of material. A full description of the methods of selection employed is to be found at the head of each of the succeeding chapters; the procedures may be briefly outlined here.

In the first investigation, that of differential fertility in the rural sections of the Mälar counties, the nativity data used were originally collected by means of birth registration. Of the three sources of error listed above as being typically associated with this form of material, the first was eliminated by the Swedish practice of assigning births to place of residence of parents, regardless of place of birth. As for the second, comparative accuracy of population figures was assured by limiting fertility computations to the two years immediately adjacent to the census date (December 31, 1930). Unfortunately the possibility of disparity in the sociological classifications of parents and of population could not be entirely eliminated, although it was considerably reduced by the fact of the common origin in the parish registers of the birth registration and the census data. (See footnote on page 36.)

In the second investigation of the present series, presented as an introductory account of differential fertility in Stockholm in 1919 to 1922, an attempt was made to eliminate entirely possible dissimilarity in the sociological classifications of births and population. Although this weakness of material seems to be inevitably associated with nativity data of the vital statistics (registration) type, it was noted above that no such defect adheres to retrospective (census) information. With retrospective material, however, new complications intrude. Fortunately the practical defects of one type of nativity data are not those of the other, so that the logical expedient is the combination of the two, uniting the best qualities of each. Thanks to the excellent organization of the Swedish population records the difficulties accompanying

this procedure are not insurmountable. In the second investigation, summarized in Chapter III below, the parents of
children born in Stockholm in the years 1919 to 1922 inclusive were identified in the 1920 census records, and the
information on birth register and census record combined.
The classification of births according to social status of
parents thus became identical with the population classification. This procedure of uniting census and registration
material will be referred to below as the »identification
method».

Finally, to consider another aspect of fertility studies: —
investigations employing registration material are necessarily cross-sectional in nature, giving a more or less instan-
taneous record of fertility. While estimates of the total fertility of marriage may be synthesized for longer periods by
combining the data for marriages of different durations at
time of observation, the results so obtained may be seriously
distorted by temporary changes in fertility produced by
brief economic and social disturbances. Information at once
more factual and more stable, in so far as temporary fluctuations of fertility are concerned, is to be had by resorting
to retrospective material. Three fundamental defects, however, were seen to be associated with the census type of
nativity data, the principal one of which was that proceeding
from changes of residence or social status between marriage
and census. If accurate information concerning possible
changes in the situation of parents is necessary, there is the
possible expedient of associating the returns of two consecutive censuses and of computing the observed fertility in
the intervening decade of married life, residence and social
status of parents being known for both the beginning and
the end of the observation period. Comparability of the social class divisions of both births and population is automatically assured by the use of retrospective material. The possibility of trend disturbance may be minimized by taking
only a given cohort of marriages, preferably those contracted just before the first of the two censuses. Restriction
of observation to the first ten years of married life presumably eliminates whatever selection there may be involved

in survival. A certain amount of selection through the moving away of families from the study area is, however, inevitable.

This »double census» method was employed in the third investigation described below, that of differential fertility in the first decade of marriage of selected Stockholm-resident families, for the period 1917 to 1930 (Chapter IV). A particular opportunity offered by this material was that of tracing the apparent effect on fertility of changing economic status. As a necessary preliminary to interpretation of the results, a fuller description and discussion of the exact procedure employed is given below (Chapter IV); the »double census» method in any case represents a further refinement of material in the study of differential fertility.


## C. Measures of Fertility.

In as much as studies of differential fertility as a rule have taken over directly the statistical techniques developed in the more general type of fertility investigation, a necessary first step in the analysis of nativity data according to social class divisions is an evaluation of the indexes of fertility available, the determination of their applicability to be made with reference to the material and the objective of the work at hand. In this connection we must clearly distinguish between two different types of fertility investigation, the one designed to measure *net reproductivity* (replacement), the other concerned with what may be called *specific fertility*. By net reproductivity is meant the observed power of a given population group to maintain or increase itself numerically, the »balance of births and deaths» to use Kuczynski's expression; it involves not only nativity but also the amount and distribution of mortality. The term specific fertility is here used to denote the observed fertility, usually expressed as births per thousand married females, under prescribed standard conditions. In terms of differential fertility, a measure of net reproductivity would therefore afford an index of the power of a given social class to increase its proportional representation in the total population through excess of births over deaths; a measure of specific fertility on the other hand would indicate the differences in fertility existing between the different social classes, all known and controllable variables other than social status being held constant.

Apart from the question of social mobility, the almost complete absence of detailed information concerning differential mortality, or mortality according to social class, has, in spite of various ingenious attempts, made impossible the exact computation of the social differential in net reproductivity. No such limitation, however, is to be found in the determination of specific fertility according to social status. In fact, much of the technique of specific fertility investigation has been developed in connection with studies of differential fertility. Researches in the field of differential fertility usually attempt to determine the specific fertility of the different social classes dealt with, arriving at an estimate of the social differential through reduction of the observed rates to a predetermined base of comparison. The investigations of differential fertility in Sweden reported below are of this type.

Although the form of the original material made it necessary to use somewhat different measures of fertility in reporting each of these investigations, the actual population base used for rate computation in each case was the number of potential mothers — the number of married women between the ages of 15 and 45. The rates so obtained for the various social classes were thus unaffected by differences in sex ratio, age distribution, and frequency of marriage.[1] Subdivision of the material gave specificity of the fertility rates according to age group of parents, duration of marriage, occupation, and so forth.

The Mälar counties data used in Chapter II gave not the number of live births but the number of reported confine-

[1] The fact that not only may the age distribution of the total and the married population vary considerably, but that even considerable differences in sex ratio may be found between occupational groups, is shown by the population figures in Tables 1 to 5 of the Appendix.

ments of married women under forty-five years of age. Stillbirths were thus included, and plural births were counted only once. While for purposes of comparison it would have been desirable to deal with live births only, confinement rates (average number of confinements per annum per thousand married women of age 15 to 44) should provide a sufficiently direct index of fertility. It is true that the element of stillbirths is thus introduced, but any uncertainty as to the exact definition of a live birth — an uncertainty somewhat complicating comparison of the published birth rates of different countries — is thereby removed. In this connection it should be noted that according to the official Swedish definition, a child is classified as born alive if showing signs of breathing at birth even if dying immediately after, and that an interruption of pregnancy before the twenty-ninth week of gestation is recorded as a miscarriage and not as a stillbirth.

In the first Stockholm study (Chapter III), fertility rates were computed from family records giving the number of live births in the period 1919 to 1922 inclusive. The total number of family-years was known for each subdivision of the material, and fertility was expressed as the average number of live births per thousand marriage years. It is to be noted that this basis of computation really corresponds to that usually employed, with fertility measured by the average number of live births per annum per thousand of average population of potential mothers, but that the rates themselves were averages for a four-year period (or less for the most recent marriages) and for different marriage duration intervals. Duration of marriage was, however, specified as well as age group of parents.

In the third of the investigations reported below (Chapter IV) the nativity data referred, not to a given calendar period of time, but to a definite marriage duration interval, the first decade of marriage. The particular technical advantage of this type of information lay in the opportunity which it gave to prepare fertility rates according to marriage year, not calendar year — the total fertility of marriage over any considerable period presumably being relatively unaffected by temporary fluctuations in fertility.[1] Furthermore, instead of using fertility rates with specification of age of mother, the age factor was separated into two components, age of wife at marriage, and duration of marriage. The original nativity data corresponded in form to those used in Chapter III.

[1] See introductory section of Chapter IV for further discussion.

# CHAPTER II.

## DIFFERENTIAL FERTILITY IN THE MÄLAR COUNTIES, 1930 AND 1931.

### A. *Fertility trends in Sweden.*

BEFORE consideration of the rather exceptional situation in Stockholm, a brief account of the relative fertility of different social classes in a rural district of Sweden is included here, both by way of general orientation and to prevent unwarranted generalization from the Stockholm observations[1]. The material to be used in this chapter, concerning nativity in the rural sections of the Mälar counties in 1930 and 1931, was obtained in a specially commissioned investigation of differential fertility in rural Sweden. In communicating these preliminary results advantage is taken of permission of the Royal Academy of Agriculture (Kungl. Lantbruksakademien).

Apart from minor fluctuations the fertility of the Swedish population, measured in terms of the average number of confinements per annum per thousand married women of childbearing age, has been falling steadily since the 1880's (Table 1), the decline being most marked in the cities but also appearing distinctly in the rates for the rural sections of the country. Computation of the per cent change in each decade shows a generally accelerating rate of decrease.

As for the rural part of the Mälar counties, the observed fertility in the last half century was consistently lower than that for rural Sweden as a whole, maintaining a position intermediate between the urban and the rural fertility

---

[1] See also Appendix B in which is given further fertility data for comparison with the Stockholm material.

**Table 1.   Confinements per annum per thousand married women age 15 to 44.**

|  | 1881—90 | 1891—00 | 1901—10 | 1911—20 | 1921—30 |
|---|---|---|---|---|---|
| Sweden, total ................... | 292 | 276 | 259 | 212 | 155 |
| » urban ................ | 278 | 240 | 223 | 166 | 1) |
| » rural ................... | 295 | 286 | 270 | 231 | 1) |
| Mälar counties, rural .......... | 267 | 252 | 229 | 190 | 142 |

averages. The downward trend was uniformly greater than that for the rest of rural Sweden. The course of the birth rate (live births per annum per thousand inhabitants) is shown in more detail in Table 2, but the relative positions are essentially the same as in the preceding tabulation.

With the exception of the years 1920 and 1930, the birth

**Table 2.   Live births per annum per thousand population.[2]**

|  | Sweden, total | Sweden, urban | Sweden, rural | Mälar count. rural |
|---|---|---|---|---|
| 1911 ........ | 24.0 | 23.8 | 24.0 | 23.8 |
| 1912 ........ | 23.7 | 23.0 | 23.9 | 23.5 |
| 1913 ........ | 23.1 | 22.3 | 23.3 | 22.3 |
| 1914 ........ | 22.9 | 21.6 | 23.3 | 22.7 |
| 1915 ........ | 21.6 | 20.2 | 22.1 | 21.3 |
| 1916 ........ | 21.1 | 19.5 | 21.8 | 21.0 |
| 1917 ........ | 20.8 | 19.3 | 21.4 | 20.6 |
| 1918 ........ | 20.3 | 17.8 | 21.3 | 20.1 |
| 1919 ........ | 19.6 | 17.3 | 20.6 | 19.6 |
| 1920 ........ | 23.6 | 21.2 | 24.6 | 23.6 |
| 1921 ........ | 21.4 | 18.8 | 22.5 | 21.5 |
| 1922 ........ | 19.6 | 16.9 | 20.7 | 19.4 |
| 1923 ........ | 18.8 | 16.1 | 20.0 | 18.5 |
| 1924 ........ | 18.1 | 15.5 | 19.2 | 17.5 |
| 1925 ........ | 17.5 | 14.9 | 18.7 | 17.0 |
| 1926 ........ | 16.9 | 14.2 | 18.1 | 16.2 |
| 1927 ........ | 16.1 | 13.2 | 17.4 | 15.2 |
| 1928 ........ | 16.0 | 13.0 | 17.4 | 15.6 |
| 1929 ........ | 15.2 | 12.4 | 16.5 | 14.3 |
| 1930 ........ | 15.4 | 12.6 | 16.7 | 14.5 |

[1] Necessary census tabulations not yet available for 1930.

[2] The Mälar county rates specially computed, the others from Sveriges officiella statistik, Folkmängden inom administrativa områden, (annual), Central Statistical Bureau, Stockholm.

rate is seen to have fallen quite steadily during the twenty year period, 1911 to 1930. During this time the total decrease in the birth rate of the Mälar counties was about forty per cent, somewhat greater than that for rural Sweden as a whole but less than the decrease in the birth rate of the total urban population.

Table 3. Average number of registered confinements per annum per thousand married women age 15 to 44, Mälar counties.

| | 15—24 | 25—29 | 30—34 | 35—39 | 40—44 | 15—44 |
|---|---|---|---|---|---|---|
| Rural, 1910—11 ........ | 405 | 295 | 229 | 173 | 88 | 216 |
| » 1930—31 ........ | 284 | 169 | 112 | 76 | 36 | 113 |
| Urban, 1910—11 ........ | 384 | 263 | 181 | 127 | 64 | 185 |
| » 1930—31 ........ | 243 | 134 | 81 | 45 | 18 | 80 |
| Decrease in per cent; rural | 29.9 | 42.7 | 51.1 | 56.1 | 59.7 | 47.7 |
| » » » » urban | 36.7 | 49.0 | 55.2 | 64.6 | 71.4 | 56.8 |

For more detailed information concerning the changes in fertility taking place between 1911 and 1930, age specific confinement rates (average number of confinements per annum per thousand married women of specified age) were computed for the Mälar district (Table 3). The rates given in the table are averages for the two-year periods, 1910 to 1911 and 1930 to 1931, inclusive; corresponding figures for the cities in the Mälar counties were included for comparison. It is to be noted that the decrease in fertility appeared at all ages, that it was without exception greater in the cities than in the country, that it was relatively least at the lower ages and greatest in the higher age groups.

## B. Description of material.

The present investigation as stated above is concerned with the rural section of the five Mälar counties; the nativity data used are those for the years 1930 and 1931, the population figures from the 1930 (Dec. 31) census.

The Mälar counties, located in central Sweden and surrounding Lake Mälar, are five in number — Stockholm,

Uppsala, Södermanland, Örebro and Västmanland. The rural population of the district in 1930 was 729,535, or 17.6 % of the total rural population of Sweden. Except for the predominantly suburban section close to the city of Stockholm the district as a whole is distinctly rural in character, relatively highly cultivated and uniformly prosperous. As compared to that of the rest of Sweden, agriculture is here characterized by the »large holding» form (storbruk), with a correspondingly high proportion of farm laborers in the population. A good many industrial centers do exist, but to the extent that they are located in the cities they are excluded from the present material.

As for what is urban and what is rural, the formal definition used in the Swedish official statistics has a purely administrative meaning. Urban districts are those chartered as cities by royal decree; all others are classified as rural regardless of size. Thus while some Swedish cities have a population of only about one thousand, certain technically rural communities have up to twenty times as many inhabitants. An arbitrary classification of political units according to size or average density of population, an expedient often employed, is of course possible but for purposes of fertility studies is not too satisfactory. In the first place, the essential criterion of ruralism is occupation — agriculture — and not size of population. In the second place, density of population is not uniform. The country districts of most civilized countries contain rather compact centers, often more urban than rural in character and perhaps with urban fertility characteristics, so that a differentiation of these communal centers from the more typically rural sections is desirable in analytic study of rural fertility.

In recognition of the need for more detailed analysis of the conditions existing in rural districts, the Royal Census Bureau in 1930 requested the parish clergy to indicate all compact villages of 200 or more inhabitants in the forthcoming parish book abstracts. With the aid of this information, checked by field investigations conducted by the Census Bureau, the Swedish census of 1930 made a division of rural communities into four groups defined as follows: —

I. communities in which at least 75 % of the 1930 population was employed, or the dependents of those employed, in one of the three essentially rural occupations, — agriculture, fishing, or the wood cutting and lumber industry.

II. communities with from 50 % to 75 % of the population dependent on these occupations.

III. communities having less than 50 % of the population dependent on these occupations, but not included in group four.

VI. Concentrated communities in which at least two-thirds of the population lived in villages of 200 or more inhabitants, but in which less than 50 % of the total number of inhabitants was assigned to the rural group of occupations.

Regardless of concentration, all communities in which at least 50 % of the inhabitants had these essentially rural occupations as a means of livelihood were assigned to one of the first two community groups. The effect of this classification, based on both occupation and concentration of population, was to give a rough grouping according to degree of ruralism or urbanization.

In the 1930 census tabulations were given two subdivisions of the population in each of the above four community groups, first according to occupation (agriculture,[1] and all others), secondly according to status in the occupation (laborers, others). The population within each of the four resulting subdivisions was further classified according to sex, age and marital status. In general a family was classified as a unit in accordance with the occupation and status of the head of the family, but in the rare cases where the wife reported an independent occupation or an occupational status different from that of the husband the two were assigned to different subdivisions of the same community group.

The essential population figures for the Mälar counties, obtained from the 1930 census, are to be found in Appendix Tables 1 and 2; summarizations of the age distribution and per cent married of the female population are given in Tables 4 and 5 of the text and in Tables 3 and 4 of the Appendix.

---

[1] The terms »agriculture», »agricultural», etc., are here used to include all three of the rural occupations.

In view of the fact that total fertility depends not only on the fertility of marriage but also on the age distribution and on the fraction of celibacy in the total population, it is noteworthy that considerable differences existed between the various community and occupational groups, as shown by the tables mentioned above. Thus, women of childbearing ages made up only about 14 % of the non-laborer agricultural population as compared to 24 % for the other occupational groups. At the same time, 87 % of the non-laborer class women of childbearing age in the agricultural population were married, in contrast to only 35 % to 45 % in the other occupational groups.

**Table 4.** **Female population age 15 to 44 in the Mälar counties, rural section, with division according to community group and occupational classification, expressed in per cent of the corresponding total population.[1]**

| Occupational classification | Community group | | | | |
|---|---|---|---|---|---|
| | I | II | III | IV | total |
| Agriculture workers ........... | 23.8 | 24.1 | 23.6 | 19.8 | 23.7 |
| »        others    ........... | 14.0 | 13.7 | 13.8 | 16.0 | 13.9 |
| »        total    ............. | 18.9 | 19.0 | 19.1 | 18.3 | 18.9 |
| Other occupations    ........... | 22.9 | 22.2 | 23.6 | 26.2 | 24.0 |
| All occupations ................ | 20.1 | 20.5 | 22.3 | 25.4 | — |

**Table 5.** **Married females age 15 to 44 in the Mälar counties, rural section, according to community group and occupational classification, expressed in per cent of the corresponding total female population age 15 to 44.[2]**

| Occupational classification | Community group | | | | |
|---|---|---|---|---|---|
| | I | II | III | IV | total |
| Agriculture workers ........... | 37.0 | 34.2 | 34.7 | 45.4 | 35.9 |
| »        others    ........... | 88.5 | 87.5 | 84.5 | 78.9 | 87.1 |
| »        total    ............. | 56.0 | 53.1 | 51.4 | 57.3 | 54.2 |
| Other occupations .............. | 32.8 | 41.8 | 47.7 | 49.7 | 45.1 |
| All occupations ................ | 48.2 | 47.4 | 48.6 | 50.3 | — |

[1] For absolute numbers and more detailed age distribution see Appendix Tables 1, 3 a, 3 b.

[2] For absolute numbers see Appendix Tables 1, 2, 4 a, 4 b.

At the request of the Royal Academy of Agriculture, tabulations parallelling those of the census data were made of the confinements registered in the Mälar counties in 1930 and 1931, the years immediately preceding and following the census date. The nativity data were obtained from the previously mentioned birth register abstracts. In the following analysis of the material so obtained the measure of fertility employed was the *confinement rate,* defined as the number of confinements per annum per thousand married women in the age group 15 to 44. All confinements reported for unmarried women and for those over 44 years of age were excluded from the material; stillbirths were included and plural births were counted only once.[1]

Under the circumstances, two of the difficulties often associated with the use of registration material (inaccurate population figures, registration of non-resident births) were avoided, but the possibility of unconformity in the social classification of parents and of total population remained. Entire uniformity in the assignment according to community group was of course obtainable, but the information as to occupation and occupational status given in the birth registers was not highly comparable to that of the census records.[2] On the whole, the classification of the nativity data into agricultural and non-agricultural groups may be considered to have been entirely reliable, but the determination of occupational status was probably less uniform, especially for the non-agricultural population. It was therefore considered advisable to use the occupational status division in the agricultural group only.

## C. *Fertility according to Community Group.*

From the 1930 and 1931 birth register abstracts was obtained record of 17,367 confinements in the rural communities of the Mälar counties, this figure including only confine-

[1] See preceding chapter for comment on the relative advantages of rates of confinements and of live births as measures of fertility.

[2] The occupational classification of the census material being based on three sources of information — parish book abstracts, annual household registration lists, annual income and property tax returns — while that of the birth registers came directly from the parish books.

ments of married women between the ages of 15 and 44 inclusive, and corresponding to an annual average of 112 confinements per thousand of the 77,148 married women, age 15 to 44, recorded in the census for December 31, 1930. (See Appendix A for illegitimate births.) Subdivision of the material was made according to community group, age of mother, occupation and occupational status (Table 5, Appendix.)

**Table 6.  Average number of confinements per annum per thousand married women in the various community groups of the rural section of the Mälar counties, 1930—1931.**

| Community group | Crude rate [1] | Confinement rates | | | | | | Standardized [2] |
|---|---|---|---|---|---|---|---|---|
| | | 15—44 | under 25 | 25—29 | 30—34 | 35—39 | 40—44 | |
| | (1) | (2) | (3) | (4) | (5) | (6) | (7) | (8) |
| I ............... | 13.3 | 137 | 329 | 205 | 132 | 99 | 45 | 137 |
| II ............... | 12.1 | 125 | 299 | 184 | 129 | 84 | 45 | 125 |
| III ............... | 11.1 | 103 | 262 | 154 | 101 | 68 | 30 | 103 |
| IV ............... | 10.7 | 84 | 234 | 131 | 84 | 52 | 21 | 84 |
| All communities .... | 11.9 | 113 | 283 | 169 | 112 | 76 | 36 | 113 |

The separate confinement rates for the four community groups (Table 6) showed a marked decrease in fertility from the more rural to the more urban communities. Essentially the same relationship held true in respect to illegitimate births (Appendix A). The relative under-fertility of the most urban of the communities was most apparent when comparison was made in terms of relatively specific rates (confinements per thousand married women of childbearing age), the higher fraction of potential mothers in this type of community partly concealing the lower fertility.

As shown by the age specific confinement rates (Table 6, columns 3 to 7 inclusive), the inverse relation of fertility to degree of urbanization appeared with regularity at all age levels and increased in relative amount with age. Standardization of the fertility rates of the different community

[1] Average number of confinements per annum per thousand population.

[2] Using as standard the age distribution of the total married female population of age 15 to 44, as given for the Mälar counties in the 1930 census.

groups with respect to age (Table 6, column 8) made no change in the relative positions, the age distributions of the potential mothers in the four community groups being similar[1] (Table 2, Appendix).

The fact of differences in fertility between the four types of communities being established by the consistent evidence of the data, the immediate question is whether or not these differences are traceable to differing compositions of the respective populations or whether they represented a more fundamental property of the various rural groups.

## D. Fertility according to Occupational Classification.

On analysis of the confinement rates according to occupation and occupational status the crude rate (confinements per annum per thousand population) for the total agricultural group (laborers and others combined) was found to be about 36 % in excess of that for the non-agricultural fraction of the population (Table 7, column 1). The computation of confinement rates, taking as base the number of potential mothers instead of the total population, increased the differential to about 43 % (Table 7, column 2). That is, the age and marital status composition of the non-agricultural population was such as to conceal its relative under-fertility.

Subdivision of the agricultural population into laborers and others demonstrated a markedly higher fertility among the former, the size of the differential again being greater when computed in terms of specific confinement rates. As was explained in the preceding chapter, no attempt was made to analyze the fertility of the non-agricultural population with respect to occupational status, the danger of disparity in the classification of nativity and population data being too actual in this particular instance to make the computed rates altogether reliable.

The differentials observed above — higher fertility of the agricultural than of the non-agricultural population, higher

[1] The standardization being with respect to age distribution in the age group 15 to 44 inclusive, it was not affected by the different proportions of potential mothers in the four population groups.

Table 7. Average number of confinements per annum per thousand women in the various occupational groups, rural section of the Mälar counties, 1930—1931.

| Occupational class | Crude rate[1] | Confinement rates[3] | | | | | | Standardized[2] |
|---|---|---|---|---|---|---|---|---|
| | | 15—44 | under 25 | 25—29 | 30—34 | 35—39 | 40—44 | |
| | (1) | (2) | (3) | (4) | (5) | (6) | (7) | (8) |
| Agriculture, workers.. | 14.4 | 169 | 352 | 213 | 148 | 110 | 51 | 148 |
| » others .. | 13.1 | 112 | 278 | 189 | 137 | 92 | 46 | 128 |
| » total .... | 14.0 | 136 | 330 | 202 | 141 | 98 | 47 | 138 |
| Other occupations .. | 10.3 | 95 | 250 | 146 | 91 | 59 | 26 | 94 |
| All occcupations .... | 11.9 | 113 | 283 | 169 | 112 | 76 | 36 | 113 |

fertility of the laborers than of the remainder of the agricultural group — persisted at all age levels (Table 7, columns 3 to 7). Of the two it was to be noted that the former tended to increase relatively with age, the latter to remain rather constant or to decrease. That is, on a relative basis the observed confinement rates of the agricultural and non-agricultural sections of the material diverged with age, while the rates for the laborer and non-laborer fractions of the agricultural group showed some tendency to converge.

To summarize: — it was found that fertility in the rural parts of the Mälar counties, as measured by the average number of confinements per thousand potential mothers, decreased from the more rural to the less rural community groups, from the more rural to the less rural occupational groups. This observation applied not only to the total popu lations but also to each age level of analysis.

## E. Fertility according to Community Group and Occupational Classification.

The average confinement rates for the two-year period of study, with specification according to community group,

[1] Average number of confinements per annum per thousand population.
[2] The standard distribution the same as in the preceding table.
[3] By use of the age and marriage distribution of Appendix Tables 3a and 4a or the original data of Appendix Tables 1 and 2, these rates may be converted to give the average number of confinements per thousand females of the given age group, or per thousand of total population.

occupational classification and age, are given in Table 8. The corresponding absolute numbers, both of population and of confinements, are to be found in Appendix Tables 2 and 5. Certain of the previously observed relations did apparently persist after this subdivision of the material, but with the resultant decrease of numbers in the various specific groups direct comparison of the computed rates was not too informative. Thus, although the population of potential mothers fell below one hundred in only two of the specific community-occupation-age groups, the computation of rates standardized according to age became necessary not only as a summarization but also for greater reliability.

The standardized confinement rates for each occupational subdivision in the four community groups are given in Table 9. The age distribution used in standardization was that of the total married female population, age 15 to 44, of the rural section of the Mälar counties. Several outstanding facts are to be noted.

1) That the occupational differential — the higher fertility of the agricultural as compared to the non-agricultural population, of the workers in the agricultural group as compared to the others — persisted after division according to community group.

2) That the occupational differential was lowest in the most rural of the community groups, highest in the most urbanized.

3) That the community differential — the higher fertility in the more rural than in the more urban communities — was much reduced by subdivision according to occupational classification, surviving only in the non-agricultural section of the population.

The evidence indicated the presence of a definite occupational status differential in fertility in the agricultural population. The existence of a real community differential in the material, however, could not be clearly established, in particular because of insufficient specificity in the occupational classification. That is, a dependable division according to occupational status could not be made for the individuals not engaged in agriculture, nor did the combination of all but

**Table 8. Average number of confinements per annum per thousand married women age 15 to 44, in specific community, occupation and age groups in the rural section of the Mälar counties 1930—1931.[1]**

| Community group | Age | Agriculture | | | Other occupations | Total |
|---|---|---|---|---|---|---|
| | | workers | others | total | | |
| I | 15—24 | 353 | 281 | 332 | 319 | 329 |
| | 25—29 | 219 | 194 | 208 | 197 | 205 |
| | 30—34 | 137 | 140 | 139 | 111 | 132 |
| | 35—39 | 109 | 99 | 102 | 87 | 99 |
| | 40—44 | 48 | 44 | 45 | 43 | 45 |
| | total | 171 | 116 | 139 | 131 | 137 |
| II | 15—24 | 351 | 283 | 330 | 264 | 299 |
| | 25—29 | 205 | 196 | 201 | 164 | 184 |
| | 30—34 | 158 | 142 | 149 | 103 | 129 |
| | 35—39 | 110 | 87 | 95 | 70 | 84 |
| | 40—44 | 58 | 53 | 54 | 32 | 45 |
| | total | 171 | 114 | 138 | 108 | 125 |
| III | 15—24 | 347 | 263 | 323 | 243 | 262 |
| | 25—29 | 210 | 172 | 194 | 141 | 154 |
| | 30—34 | 156 | 120 | 136 | 90 | 101 |
| | 35—39 | 114 | 86 | 97 | 57 | 68 |
| | 40—44 | 44 | 36 | 38 | 26 | 30 |
| | total | 164 | 100 | 129 | 94 | 103 |
| IV | 15—24 | 356 [2] | 250 [2] | 325 | 226 | 234 |
| | 25—29 | 213 | 138 | 184 | 126 | 131 |
| | 30—34 | 151 | 104 | 128 | 80 | 84 |
| | 35—39 | 113 | 85 | 97 | 48 | 52 |
| | 40—44 | 58 | 35 | 45 | 18 | 21 |
| | total | 159 | 90 | 125 | 80 | 84 |
| All communities | 15—24 | 352 | 278 | 330 | 250 | 283 |
| | 25—29 | 213 | 189 | 202 | 146 | 169 |
| | 30—34 | 148 | 137 | 141 | 91 | 112 |
| | 35—39 | 110 | 92 | 98 | 59 | 76 |
| | 40—44 | 51 | 46 | 47 | 26 | 36 |
| | total | 169 | 112 | 136 | 95 | 113 |

[1] Rates convertible as were those of the two preceding tables by use of appropriate data in Appendix Tables 1—4 inclusive.

[2] Rate based on data for less than 100 married women.

**Table 9. Confinement rates of the occupational groups in each type of community, standardized with respect to age distribution.** [1]

| Community group | Agriculture | | | Other occupations | All communities |
|---|---|---|---|---|---|
| | workers | others | total | | |
| I ............ | 147 | 132 | 140 | 126 | 137 |
| II ............ | 150 | 131 | 140 | 105 | 125 |
| III ............ | 149 | 117 | 134 | 92 | 103 |
| IV ............ | 150 | 103 | 129 | 80 | 84 |
| All communities | 148 | 128 | 138 | 94 | 113 |

the essentially rural occupations give a sufficiently homogeneous occupation group. As a result the non-agricultural population of the most rural communities may have been very different from that of the more concentrated and industrial communities, and the community group differential observed in the fertility of the non-agricultural class of population, therefore, may very well have been due to differences in the composition of the population rather than to any direct association of community type and fertility.

Similarly, the greater divergence of the fertility rates of the two agricultural subdivisions in the more concentrated communities than in the more typically rural districts may have merely reflected a more definite distinction between the two occupational status groups. That this may actually have been the case was suggested by a comparison of the ratio of adult agricultural workers to the total agricultural population, the fraction of workers rising steadily from community group I to community group IV. The same phenomenon of an increasing fraction of workers was also to be observed in the non-agricultural population. It may well be that whatever decrease in fertility was observed, going from the more rural to the more urbanlike communities, was fictitious and due to a changing class definition or alteration in relative social status.

[1] Using the same age distribution for standard as in Tables 6 and 7.

## F.  Summary.

Analysis was made of the fertility of the Mälar counties' rural population in the years 1930 and 1931, the measure of fertility used being a confinement rate, the number of registered confinements per thousand married women between the ages of fifteen and forty-five.

A primary division of the material was made classifying the technically rural communities into four groups according to degree of ruralism, information as to occupational distribution and concentration of population providing the basis of classification.

The population in each of these four community groups was further divided according to occupation (rural occupations, others) and occupational status (workers, others). Confinement rates were computed for each of these subgroups, with specification of age of mother. All comparisons were made in terms of either age specific or age standardized rates. The following were the principal observations.

1) With analysis according to community group, fertility was found to decrease steadily from the more rural to the more urban communities.

2) With analysis according to occupational classification, fertility was found to be higher for the rural than for the non-rural occupation groups, higher for the laborers than for others assigned to the rural occupations.

3) These occupational differentials in fertility persisted after simultaneous division of the material according to both community group and occupational classification. While the community group differential was not entirely eliminated by this method of analysis, it was considerably reduced, surviving only in the non-rural occupations.

These observations must be interpreted with regard for two technical defects of the primary material: — first, lack of information as to duration of marriage; second, lack of assured uniformity in the occupational classification of nativity data and population. Thus, the observed fertility differentials were affected by the factor of marriage duration, and therefore did not directly measure differences in specific fertility. Furthermore, even though the error arising from the lack of absolute uniformity in occupational classification was probably negligible within a given community group, the significance of the occupational categories may well have changed with type of community.

It is therefore not improbable that the community differential remaining after subdivision according to occupational groups was attributable to the presence of a different class of inhabitants in the more urbanized of the rural communities rather than to any real relation of community type and fertility, and that occupation and occupational status are more fundamental variables than community type in the study of differential fertility.

# CHAPTER III.

## FERTILITY OF STOCKHOLM FAMILIES, 1919—1922.

### A. Description of material.

IN studies of differential fertility, where analysis is made of the fertility characteristics of various population strata or social classes, many different social criteria have been used in classification but quite regardless of the definition of social class, whether based on income, occupation or education, the fertility differentials observed have been entirely consistent in direction if not in amount. Fertility has been found to be highest in the lower classes, lowest in the better situated population groups, however these may have been defined. It has therefore become practically axiomatic that human fertility is inversely related to social status. In recent years, however, a few reports of apparent reversals of the fertility differentials have appeared[1]; of these both the earliest and the most authentic have come from a series of investigations of differential fertility in Stockholm.[2] It is the object of this and the following chapter to make a critical

[1] For a review of the available literature on this subject see Lorimer and Osborn, »Dynamics of Population», Macmillan, New York, 1934.

[2] K. A. Edin: (1) »Vårt moderna Befolkningsproblem», Sexuell Hygien, pp. 80—93, Almquist and Wicksell, Uppsala, 1927. (2) Proceedings of the World Population Conference, 1927. Pp. 205—207, Arnold, London 1928. (3) »The Birth Rate Changes», Eugenics Review, 1929, XX, pp. 258—266. (4) »Födelsekontrollens Inträngande hos de breda Lagren», Ekonomisk Tidskrift 1929, pp 123—152. (5) »The Fertility of the Social Classes in Stockholm in the years 1919—1929», Proceedings of the Second General Assembly of the International Union for the Scientific Investigation of Population Problems, pp. 91—101, Allen and Unwin, London 1932. (6) »Bidrag till Befolkningsstatistikens Metodik», Statsvetenskaplig Tidskrift, pp. 245—264, 409—425, 1933. Of these, the first four articles reported various aspects of the investigation reviewed in Chapter III below.

survey of this Stockholm material, and to present a somewhat more detailed analysis than was possible in the earlier publications.

It was noted in the preceding chapter that two fundamental weaknesses existed in the Mälar counties material, — unknown duration of marriage and some uncertainty as to the uniformity in occupational classification of nativity data and population. In the investigation to be reviewed below, concerned with differential fertility in Stockholm in the years 1919 to 1922 inclusive, these two defects were avoided in selecting the primary material.

From the 1920 census records, separate cards were made out for each family registered as resident in Greater Stockholm[1] on December 31, 1920. Only the families in which husband and wife were living together were included, and only those in which the wife was less than forty years old at date of census (born 1881 or after). A total of slightly over 39,000 family cards was thus obtained. The records of all children born in Greater Stockholm in the years 1919 to 1922 inclusive were abstracted from the parish birth registers, the material being refined to include only legitimate births to women born after 1880 and married previous to 1921. The mothers were then identified in the census material and the nativity data transferred to the family cards. Practically all the mothers entered in the birth registers could be so identified, the process of identification being simplified by the completeness of information on the birth records.

The data thus obtained combined retrospective (census) and registration material. The method of collection was the »identification method» referred to previously. As compared to the Mälar counties investigation of the preceding chapter, the sample of material covered was more selected but in compensation was susceptible of more fundamental analysis. In particular the sociological classification of births and of population was of assured uniformity.

[1] Including besides Stockholm proper the cities Lidingö, Sundbyberg, Djursholm; the towns Hässelby, Stocksund and Saltsjöbaden; also Solna, Spånga, Danderyd and Nacka parishes.

The measure of fertility used was the number of live births per thousand years of married life. In computing the total number of years, the 1919 marriages were assigned a »risk period» of three and one-half years, the 1920 marriages two and one-half years; families formed previous to 1919 contributed four years' nativity experience between 1919 and 1922 inclusive. The total number of years of married life covered in the study was 150,400.

During the study period, families could enter the sample not only by marriage but also by moving to Stockholm in the years 1919 and 1920, but in this case information was to be had from the census records concerning living children and date of birth. Children born in 1919 or 1920 but dying before removal of parents to Stockholm were not represented in the material, but could not have been sufficiently numerous to produce any appreciable disturbance of rates. A more actual possibility of error was removal of families from the childbearing population but not from the family card file, this either by separation of parents or by moving away from Stockholm between census and end of the study period. As a check on this source of error, records of the Stockholm Municipal Registration Office (Mantalskontoret) were examined; it was found that allowance for the removals in 1921 and 1922 reduced the computed total of years of married life by about 1.5 %. This change being comparatively slight and showing no association with social status, no correction for it was made in computing rates of fertility.

In tabulation, subdivision of the material was made according to sex of child, age of parents on December 31, 1920, occupation of father, date of marriage of parents (1920, 1919, 1916—1918, before 1916), income of father in 1920 (under 4,000 kronor[1] per annum, 4—6,000, 6—10,000, 10,000 or more), residence (district of city), birthplace of parents (in Greater Stockholm, elsewhere) and employment of wife. In the latter case, wives were classified as employed if reporting earned income of 300 or more kronor in 1920. For the women married in 1920, information

[1] Par value of the krona is about 1 s. 1½ d., $0.266.

was collected concerning births occurring shortly before or after marriage. Stillbirths were recorded although not included in the computation of fertility rates; information was also had concerning the number of children dying within the first year of life.

**Table 10. Fertility in Stockholm, 1919 to 1922: average number of live births per thousand years of married life, with division according to age of parents at the 1920 census and period of marriage.[1]**

| Age of husband | Under 35 | | | 35 or over | | | Total | | |
|---|---|---|---|---|---|---|---|---|---|
| Age of wife | —30 | 30—39 | total | —30 | 30—39 | total | —30 | 30—39 | total |
| Marriage 1919—20... | 268 | 172 | 247 | 261 | 162 | 200 | 267 | 168 | 237 |
| 1916—18... | 177 | 141 | 165 | 184 | 131 | 148 | 178 | 137 | 160 |
| before 1916... | 106 | 85 | 92 | 108 | 63 | 65 | 107 | 68 | 74 |
| Total | 189 | 111 | 154 | 166 | 74 | 84 | 185 | 86 | 119 |

In preliminary analysis of the fertility differentials, initial distinction must be made between the sociological variables and the various other factors which are known to affect fertility directly. The sociological variables available for analysis included residence, income, occupational group, and birthplace of parents. Evaluation of the corresponding social differentials was necessarily made with control of the variables of the second type (such as age of husband and wife, and duration of marriage). That is, even though the fertility rates used in comparisons were themselves relatively specific, being in terms of live births per thousand years of married life, the additional factors of age of parents and duration of marriage must be considered. An initial analysis of the non-sociological variables was therefore made in order to find their relative significance in relation to fertility in the particular material dealt with.

In Table 10 are the observed fertility rates according to cross tabulations of age of wife, age of husband, and duration of marriage. The following relations are apparent.

1) Duration of marriage: as is to be expected, one of

[1] Original data in Appendix Table 6.

the major variables, whether judged by the total rates (last column, Table 10) or by the individual vertical series.

2) Age of wife: for the combined material, fertility of the younger wives more than double that of the older wives; the differential reduced in the more specific groups but entirely consistent in direction.

3) Age of husband: of less importance than the two other variables but apparently with some relation to fertility.

Control of at least the first two of these variables is therefore a necessary preliminary to comparison of the fertility of different social groups in the Stockholm material.

As regards the sociological variables, attention will be confined to income and occupation, preliminary analysis according to district of city and birthplace of parents having shown little of immediate interest.

## B. *Fertility and Income Group.*

Classification according to annual income was made using reported income of husband in 1920, not total family income. The original sources of this information were the 1920 income tax returns which were incorporated into the census material as described above. As for accuracy, the reported incomes may be considered to have been highly reliable, individual income statements being checked with the pay roll lists required from all employers. Divisions were made at 4,000, at 6,000 and at 10,000 kronor per annum, giving a total of four income groups. Interpretation of these income categories, however, is not readily made. Only approximate occupational equivalents can be given since, in general, wages for the more skilled grades of labor run comparatively high while minor clerical and »white collar» positions are relatively poorly paid. The lowest income group, under 4,000 kronor, includes not only the unemployed and the intermittently employed but also a large fraction of the wage-earning population. Of the total number of years of married life in this group, over one-half was contributed by the families of laborers and industrial workers, much of the rest presumably coming from such occupational groups as sales

4

personnel, clerical staff, etc. For the 4—6,000 kronor division somewhat less than one-half of the total of marriage years were contributed by the families of laborers and industrial workers. Also included were presumably some office and business staff, minor officials, and some individuals with small independent incomes. Between 6,000 and 10,000 come a few skilled laborers, some public officials, small proprietors and the moderately well-to-do. At an income of 10,000 or over come independent business men, professional men, the higher managerial staff, etc.

Interpretation of whatever apparent associations may be found between fertility and income is also rendered more difficult by the abnormal economic conditions during the study period, 1919 to 1922 inclusive.[1] The first two years witnessed a sharp upward swing of the business cycle, — industrial activity, prices and wages rising rapidly, unemployment falling to a minimum. The following business depression, beginning at about the end of 1920, developed even more rapidly, unemployment rates abruptly increasing in most trades from December, 1920 and reaching a maximum about a year later, prices and total wages falling. Real wages, which had been rising gradually but steadily for some years, showed the customary lag, continuing an upward swing into 1921, and falling slightly thereafter.

From the point of view economics, therefore, the four year interval was sharply and equally divided into a period of abnormal business activity and a period of rapid deflation. A coincident increase in the birth rate is to be noted (Table 2), perhaps causally related to the 1920 peak of the business cycle, perhaps a post-war phenomenon. Even assuming direct association of fertility and income, however, entire agreement of birth rate curve and indexes of prosperity is not to be expected, if only because of the lag imposed by the considerable interval between conception and birth.

At least two other influences may have operated to delay the response of birth rates to economic fluctuations. In the

[1] It should be noted also that an acute housing shortage existed in Stockholm around 1920.

first place, it is to be noted that the fluctuation of real wages and of purchasing power in Sweden was neither relatively great nor abrupt between 1919 and 1922, in part due to a rather general system of adjusting wage scales according to cost of living indexes.

In the second place, it is possible that there was a temporary carry-over of optimism from the peak of the business cycle, and that actual fertility was determined somewhat by expectations as well as by present income. In such a case (and on assumption of an appreciable amount of premeditation), a socio-economic differential in fertility should appear, the classes with stable and assured income being affected less or later by economic disturbances.

Evidence has been found elsewhere of some correlation between business cycles and birth rates, but with a lag of two or three years[1]; there are also various special circumstances, as noted, which indicate that the fertility rates observed in Stockholm in 1919 to 1922 were not necessarily strongly affected by the coincident economic disturbance. The fact remains, however, that this particular period was abnormal in more than one respect, and that allowance for this abnormality must be made in interpretation of the observed fertility differentials. It is to be hoped that a special study of the Stockholm material may be made later from a socio-economic viewpoint, but for the present the four-year period will be treated as a unit, and the simple classification according to the 1920 income of husband followed.

The observed fertility rates of the four income groups, with specification of age of parents and duration of marriage, are given in Table 11. In spite of the many divisions of the material, subgroups did not become seriously small (see Appendix, Table 6); in only a few cases were the fertility rates based on fewer than five hundred years of experience, these exceptions being confined to the most recent marriage group which contained only a two-year cohort of marriages.

The rates (Table 11) for the various marriage duration

[1] Dorothy Swaine Thomas: »Social Aspects of the Business Cycle», pp. 97—100. Routledge. London, 1925.

Table 11. Live births per thousand years of married life for the different income classes in Stockholm, 1919 to 1922, according to age of parents at the 1920 census and period of marriage.[1]

| Age of husband ........ | Under 35 | | | 35 or over | | | Total | | |
|---|---|---|---|---|---|---|---|---|---|
| Age of wife : ........... | —30 | 30—39 | total | —30 | 30—39 | total | —30 | 30—39 | total |
| *Income under 4,000 kronor* | | | | | | | | | |
| Marriage 1919—20... | 270 | 158 | 246 | 255[2] | 147 | 181 | 269 | 153 | 234 |
| 1916—18... | 156 | 128 | 147 | 162 | 107 | 122 | 157 | 120 | 141 |
| before 1916... | 98 | 75 | 83 | 112 | 58 | 61 | 101 | 63 | 69 |
| Total | 183 | 102 | 148 | 161 | 69 | 79 | 180 | 82 | 118 |
| *Income 4—6,000 kronor* | | | | | | | | | |
| Marriage 1919—20... | 268 | 175 | 247 | 212 | 166 | 182 | 263 | 172 | 235 |
| 1916—18... | 171 | 130 | 156 | 150 | 121 | 129 | 168 | 127 | 150 |
| before 1916... | 98 | 78 | 84 | 92 | 57 | 59 | 96 | 63 | 68 |
| Total | 182 | 102 | 145 | 135 | 67 | 74 | 175 | 80 | 112 |
| *Income 6—10,000 kronor* | | | | | | | | | |
| Marriage 1916—20... | 245 | 185 | 232 | 308[1] | 174 | 234 | 255 | 180 | 232 |
| 1916—18... | 188 | 169 | 181 | 210 | 139 | 163 | 193 | 156 | 175 |
| before 1916... | 121 | 105 | 109 | 91 | 63 | 64 | 111 | 72 | 77 |
| Total | 192 | 132 | 163 | 185 | 74 | 87 | 190 | 91 | 119 |
| *Income 10,000 kronor or over* | | | | | | | | | |
| Marriage 1919—20... | 301 | 216[2] | 283 | 297[2] | 178[2] | 238 | 299 | 193 | 265 |
| 1916—18... | 260 | 204 | 242 | 232 | 185 | 203 | 252 | 193 | 226 |
| before 1916... | 163 | 130 | 140 | 140 | 81 | 86 | 150 | 88 | 96 |
| Total | 249 | 160 | 209 | 201 | 95 | 112 | 231 | 108 | 142 |

groups give the observed fertilities at different periods of marriage, the rates for the 1919 and 1920 marriages referring on the average to the first two and one-half or three and one-half years, the rates for the 1916 to 1918 group being the average fertility in a four-year period beginning on the average from one-half to two and one-half years after marriage, and so forth. It is to be noted that the income class differentials were least, relatively, in the first

[1] Total years of married life and number of live births for each subgroup to be found in Appendix Table 6; rates for total in Table 10 of text.

[2] Rate based on less than 500 marriage years.

years of marriage, and that the superior fertility of the families with greater income was most apparent in the later years. In other words, the active childbearing in the latter classes appears to have spread over a longer period of years.

For more direct comparison, standardized fertility rates were computed for each income class, this eliminating differences in age composition and marriage duration. The age and marriage year distribution of the total material was taken as standard, weights being assigned on the basis of the total number of years of married life contributed by each subgroup rather than on the basis of the number of families.

| Standardization | Income Class | | | |
|---|---|---|---|---|
| | under 4,000 | 4—6.000 | 6—10,000 | 10,000 or over |
| For marriage duration only | 110 | 112 | 124 | 153 |
| For age of parents only .. | 112 | 110 | 125 | 157 |
| For both age of parents and marriage duration.... | 110 | 112 | 125 | 159 |
| Unstandardized | 118 | 112 | 119 | 142 |

With elimination of differences in internal composition of the income classes, the positive correlation of fertility and income becomes more apparent, differences in age distribution and in the proportion of recent marriages having exaggerated the fertility of the lower income classes and partially concealed the greater specific fertility at the higher income levels. Actually, marriage is known to occur generally at a somewhat earlier age in the lower social classes, but under the circumstances it is not possible to say whether the poorer fraction of the Stockholm population typically exhibits a greater than average proportion of recent marriages. The observed situation as regards distribution of marriage durations may have been only a temporary one, but the outcome of standardization demonstrated the desirability of controlling marriage duration before attempting to isolate specific fertility differentials.

The unstandardized rates in the above tabulation were not

without special interest, showing as they did that the greater
fertility of the upper income groups was not merely an artifact of standardization, but that even with the handicap of
later and longer marriages, the families with higher income
also had the higher absolute fertility.

A further check on the validity of the observed positive
correlation between fertility and income could be made with
the material at hand. It will be recalled that information was
to be had concerning employment or non-employment of
wife, earned income in 1920 being used as a criterion of
employment. Although essentially a sociological variable,
employment may have a very direct and automatic effect on
fertility.[1] Separate fertility rates were accordingly prepared
for the three lower income groups, with inclusion only of
the data for families in which the wife was not employed
(reporting earned income of less than 300 kronor) in 1920.
Employment of wife was so rare in the highest income group

**Table 12. Live births per thousand years of married life, families
in which the wife reported earned income of less than 300 kronor
in 1920.** [2]

| Income kronor | Age of husband .............. | Under 35 | | 35 or over | |
|---|---|---|---|---|---|
| | Age of wife ................. | under 30 | 30—39 | under 30 | 30—39 |
| Under 4,000 | Marriage 1919—20 ...... | 293 | 187 | 265 | 169 |
| | 1916—18 ...... | 171 | 143 | 174 | 118 |
| | before 1916 ...... | 110 | 83 | 124 | 64 |
| | Total | 198 | 114 | 173 | 76 |
| 4—6,000 | Marriage 1919—20 ...... | 284 | 183 | 231 [3] | 199 |
| | 1916—18 ...... | 184 | 143 | 159 | 135 |
| | before 1916 ...... | 107 | 82 | 99 | 62 |
| | Total | 192 | 108 | 143 | 73 |
| 6—10,000 | Marriage 1919—20 ...... | 260 | 201 [3] | 314 [3] | 178 [3] |
| | 1916—18 ...... | 197 | 177 | 215 | 149 |
| | before 1916 ...... | 122 | 108 | 95 | 64 |
| | Total | 198 | 135 | 187 | 76 |

[1] That is, its influence may not be limited to inducing voluntary limitation
of number of births; it may also operate to actually reduce reproductive
power.

[2] Absolute numbers in Appendix Table 7.

[3] Rates based on less than 500 marriage years.

that no adjustment for it was necessary in making comparisons.

The fertility rates of the non-employed wives in the three lower income groups are given in Table 12. With these rates standardization was made according to marriage duration and age of parents, using the same weights as before. The standard fertilities so obtained were 121 for the lowest income class, 120 with 4—6,000 kronor income, 130 with income of between 6,000 and 10,000, these to be compared to 159 for the highest income category (see preceding tabulation of standardized fertility rates). That is, the income class fertility differential was somewhat reduced but persisted even with comparison confined to the data for non-employed wives.

The exact significance of this is not too obvious. Neither income nor employment are simple variables, and subdivision of a given income group according to employment of wife probably entails a concealed classification according to social and economic status. In any case it was apparent on examination of the data that the working wives characteristically had a relative under-fertility, whether or not this was due to the employment *per se*. Although a higher incidence of employment of wife may be an integral element of the lower income social complex, elimination of this factor gave assurance that the fertility of the poorer classes was presented as favorably as possible and that the greater fertility of the better situated Stockholm families was not merely apparent but real.

To summarize: analysis of intramarital fertility rates was made according to reported income of husband in 1920, the income groupings used being four in number, — under 4,000 kronor, 4—6,000 kronor, 6—10,000 kronor, and at least 10,000 kronor per annum. Comparison was made with standardization according to age of husband, age of wife, and duration of marriage. Fertility, expressed as average number of live births per thousand years of married life, increased from the lowest to the highest income groups. This relation persisted when comparison was confined to the fertility rates of the non-employed wives.

The evidence was entirely consistent that the observed income class differentials in fertility were not produced by any bias in the data, and that the intramarital fertility in Stockholm, 1919 to 1922, was greater in the upper than in the lower income classes.

## C. Occupation and Income.

Classification of the Stockholm families was also made according to occupation of the husband in 1920, the necessary information being obtained from the census records. Occupation does in general provide an excellent basis for social classification, giving a considerable unity in many social factors; at the same time, however, within a given industry there may occur wide variation in type of work and in economic status. With the Stockholm material the most significant scheme of analysis was judged to be a combination of occupational and income classification, as recommended by Lorimer and Osborn.[1] The income categories were the same as in the preceding section; the occupational groups used were four in number: —

A. Industry, workers; including workers in the printing, textile, chemical, food products, and building industries, as well as unskilled day labor.

B. Industry, others; including technicians, overseers, office staff.

C. Trade and commerce; including employees of wholesale and retail stores, banks, hotels, restaurants, telephone and telegraph service, transportation.

D. Arts and professions; including also state and municipal employees, army and naval officers, hospital staff.

Fertility rates were computed for each of these occupational groups with subdivision according to income of husband in 1920, duration of marriage, and age of wife, the average number of live births per thousand years of married life again being used as the measure of fertility (Table 13). Division according to age of father was omitted. With this subdivision of the material the numbers became rather small

[1] Op. cit., p. 55.

in certain categories, as may be seen from the appendix tabulations of the original data (Table 8). The industrial groups in particular were poorly represented above the 6,000 kronor level, but the results obtained were on the whole consistent.

The items of immediate interest were the two sociological variables, occupation and income. As with the above analysis according to income alone, it was of particular interest to note the relative fertilities of the various specific occupation-income groups at different periods of marriage, the necessary information being given by the fertility rates for the different marriage durations (Table 13). In accord with previous observations, the social differentials were found to be least, on a relative basis, in the first years of marriage. The greater fertility of the better situated classes appeared most strongly in the later years of marriage.

To assist in cross-comparison, standardization with respect to age of wife and marriage duration was made for each occupation-income subgroup of Table 13, the distribution of the total material again being used as standard. From the standardized rates, Table 14, it appeared that income, not occupation, was the significant variable as regards fertility. With the exception of group A (industrial workers) the fertility rates of the occupational groups differed comparatively little and increased similarly from the lowest to the highest income category. The industrial workers only were different, having not only the lowest average fertility but also an inverse relation of fertility to income.

The above observations are unusual, not only because of the general reversal of the income differential from that customarily found, but also in the absence of considerable differences between the standardized fertility rates of the occupational groups, group A excepted. Studies of fertility employing occupational classifications typically demonstrate the existence of considerable differentials. Detailed classification according to occupation, however, does involve classification according to economic as well as social status, and further analysis according to income is unfortunately seldom attempted. The absence of marked fertility differences between the occupational groups, B, C, and D, may admittedly be attributed to insufficient specificity in the occupational classification; it may also be a result of the reduction of comparison to a relatively specific basis, employing intramarital fertility rates with equalization of the factors of duration of marriage, age of wife, and income.

As in the preceding analysis of the income differential, separate fertility rates for the occupation-income groups were computed with inclusion only of the data for non-employed wives. Again, this was perhaps an over-refinement of analysis; just as differences in economic status are inextricably associated with occupation groups, a varying rate of employment of wives may also be an essential sociological component of the occupational variable. In justice to the material and in view of the somewhat unusual character of

**Table 13. Live births per thousand years of married life: fertility of Stockholm families, 1919 to 1922, according to occupational group, income of husband in 1920, age of wife at the 1920 census and period of marriage.**

| Income kronor | Occupation group...... Age of wife ......... | Group A | | | Group B | | |
|---|---|---|---|---|---|---|---|
| | | under 30 | 30—39 | total | under 30 | 30—39 | total |
| Under 4,000 | Marriage 1919—20 | 276 | 167 | 240 | 224[2] | 133[2] | 189 |
| | 1916—18 | 151 | 124 | 139 | 175 | 119 | 150 |
| | before 1916 | 100 | 64 | 70 | 113[2] | 55 | 64 |
| | Total | 175 | 83 | 114 | 173 | 74 | 108 |
| 4—6,000 | Marriage 1919—20 | 256 | 182 | 232 | 264 | 169[2] | 233 |
| | 1916—18 | 158 | 116 | 139 | 181 | 146 | 167 |
| | before 1916 | 85 | 64 | 67 | 114 | 67 | 74 |
| | Total | 159 | 79 | 103 | 187 | 89 | 124 |
| 6—10,000 | Marriage 1919—20 | 247[2] | 163[2] | 221[2] | 224[2] | 179[2] | 209 |
| | 1916—18 | 144[2] | 117[2] | 132 | 203 | 150 | 179 |
| | before 1916 | 83[2] | 64 | 67 | 127[2] | 74 | 80 |
| | Total | 143 | 74 | 93 | 188 | 91 | 120 |
| 10,000 or over | Marriage 1919—20 | — | — | — | 322[2] | 165[2] | 264 |
| | 1916—18 | — | — | — | 250 | 175[2] | 219 |
| | before 1916 | — | — | — | 124[3] | 92 | 96 |
| | Total | — | — | — | 226 | 105 | 137 |
| Total | Marriage 1919—20 | 266 | 173 | 235 | 249 | 159 | 218 |
| | 1916—18 | 154 | 120 | 139 | 200 | 146 | 177 |
| | before 1916 | 91 | 64 | 68 | 119 | 73 | 79 |
| | Total | 166 | 80 | 107 | 191 | 90 | 122 |

Table 13 continued. [1]

| Income (kronor) | Occupation group / Age of wife | Group C under 30 | Group C 30—39 | Group C total | Group D under 30 | Group D 30—39 | Group D total |
|---|---|---|---|---|---|---|---|
| Under 4,000 | Marriage 1919—20 | 261 | 170 | 235 | 285 | 89[2] | 239 |
| | 1916—18 | 154 | 111 | 135 | 172 | 123 | 153 |
| | before 1916 | 105 | 65 | 71 | 89[2] | 63 | 68 |
| | Total | 180 | 83 | 120 | 203 | 80 | 137 |
| 4—6,000 | Marriage 1919—20 | 261 | 165 | 230 | 273 | 162 | 243 |
| | 1916—18 | 180 | 135 | 161 | 169 | 128 | 152 |
| | before 1916 | 109 | 62 | 70 | 102 | 61 | 67 |
| | Total | 187 | 83 | 119 | 185 | 79 | 117 |
| 6—10,000 | Marriage 1919—20 | 267 | 192[2] | 249 | 267 | 175[2] | 234 |
| | 1916—18 | 188 | 170 | 180 | 215 | 157 | 185 |
| | before 1916 | 125[2] | 78 | 83 | 106 | 70 | 74 |
| | Total | 202 | 102 | 135 | 200 | 89 | 117 |
| 10,000 or over | Marriage 1919—20 | 296 | 207[2] | 266 | 294[2] | 196[2] | 267 |
| | 1916—18 | 255 | 200 | 231 | 248 | 194 | 223 |
| | before 1916 | 164 | 84 | 96 | 148 | 90 | 97 |
| | Total | 236 | 109 | 147 | 228 | 108 | 140 |
| Total | Marriage 1919—20 | 266 | 177 | 240 | 278 | 153 | 243 |
| | 1916—18 | 187 | 146 | 169 | 191 | 146 | 171 |
| | before 1916 | 122 | 71 | 78 | 110 | 70 | 76 |
| | Total | 196 | 92 | 128 | 199 | 88 | 125 |

Table 14. Standardized fertility rates of the four occupational groups in Stockholm, 1919 to 1922, with subdivision according to income class and with standardization of distribution of age of wife and marriage period.

| Income (kronor) | Group A | Group B | Group C | Group D | Total |
|---|---|---|---|---|---|
| Under 4,000.... | 111 | 104 | 110 | 110 | 110 |
| 4—6000......... | 109 | 120 | 115 | 112 | 112 |
| 6—10,000 ...... | 105 | 125 | 131 | 127 | 125 |
| 10,000 or over.. | — | 152 | 154 | 154 | 154 |
| Total | 110 | 124 | 124 | 123 | |
| Unstandardized total | 107 | 122 | 128 | 125 | |

[1] Absolute numbers in Appendix Table 8.

[2] Rates based on less than 500 marriage years.

**Table 15. Live births per thousand years of married life; fertility in 1919 to 1922 of Stockholm families in which the wife reported less than 300 kronor earned income in 1920, with division by occupational group, marriage period, income, and age of wife at the 1920 census** [1]

| Income (kronor) | Occupation group .... | Group A | | | Group B | | |
|---|---|---|---|---|---|---|---|
| | Age of wife ......... | under 30 | 30—39 | total | under 30 | 30—39 | total |
| Under 4,000 | Marriage 1919—20 | 301 | 196 | 268 | 219[2] | 156[2] | 198 |
| | 1916—18 | 168 | 143 | 157 | 191 | 132[2] | 164 |
| | before 1916 | 116 | 73 | 79 | 121[2] | 56 | 68 |
| | Total | 193 | 94 | 128 | 179 | 78 | 113 |
| 4—6,000 | Marriage 1919—20 | 273 | 208 | 252 | 274[2] | 180[2] | 245 |
| | 1916—18 | 173 | 130 | 154 | 195 | 154 | 179 |
| | before 1916 | 93 | 71 | 75 | 121[2] | 67 | 76 |
| | Total | 169 | 87 | 112 | 196 | 89 | 127 |
| 6,000 or over | Marriage 1919—20 | 253[2] | 175[2] | 229[2] | 266 | 176[2] | 236 |
| | 1916—18 | 160[2] | 122[2] | 142 | 229 | 172 | 206 |
| | before 1916 | 88[2] | 68 | 71 | 128 | 84 | 89 |
| | Total | 153 | 79 | 98 | 209 | 99 | 130 |

**Table 15 continued.** [1]

| Income (kronor) | Occupation group .... | Group C | | | Group D | | |
|---|---|---|---|---|---|---|---|
| | Age of wife ......... | under 30 | 30—39 | total | under 30 | 30—39 | total |
| Under 4,000 | Marriage 1919—20 | 286 | 195[2] | 262 | 306 | 94[2] | 262 |
| | 1916—18 | 165 | 118 | 144 | 182 | 132 | 162 |
| | before 1916 | 113 | 69 | 76 | 92[2] | 67 | 72 |
| | Total | 192 | 88 | 127 | 212 | 85 | 143 |
| 4—6,000 | Marriage 1919—20 | 268 | 175 | 240 | 295 | 179[2] | 266 |
| | 1916—18 | 191 | 150 | 173 | 179 | 143 | 165 |
| | before 1916 | 118 | 67 | 74 | 111 | 63 | 70 |
| | Total | 195 | 88 | 125 | 196 | 83 | 124 |
| 6,000 or over | Marriage 1919—20 | 289 | 208[2] | 266 | 293 | 195[2] | 264 |
| | 1916—18 | 226 | 191 | 211 | 238 | 177 | 209 |
| | before 1916 | 149 | 83 | 92 | 130 | 80 | 86 |
| | Total | 222 | 108 | 144 | 217 | 98 | 129 |

[1] Original data in Appendix, Table 9.
[2] Rates based on less than 500 marriage years.

Table 16. Standardized fertility rates of the four occupational groups in Stockholm, 1919 to 1922, for families in which the wife reported less than 300 kronor earned income in 1920, with subdivision according to income class and standardization according to age of wife and marriage period.

| Income (kronor) | Group A | Group B | Group C | Group D |
|---|---|---|---|---|
| Under 4,000...... | 126 | 110 | 118 | 117 |
| 4—6,000 ........ | 120 | 125 | 123 | 120 |
| 6,000 or over .... | 111 | 140 | 147 | 144 |
| Total | 122 | 129 | 131 | 130 |
| Unstandardized total | 117 | 125 | 133 | 129 |

the observations above, however, it was desirable to carry examination of the occupation and income differentials of fertility as far as possible, and to give assurance that the inversion of fertility differentials from the usual order was not produced by peculiarities in the internal composition of the sample studied.

The fertility rates of the non-employed wives in the various occupation-income groups are in Table 15, the scheme of tabulation parallelling that of Table 13 except for the combination of the two highest income groups found necessary with this division of the material. This refinement, excluding the data for employed wives, is seen to have merely increased the specific fertility rates with little change in the relative positions. For more direct comparison of the occupation and income group fertilities, standardization with respect to age of mother and marriage duration was made, using the same weights as before. The standardized rates so obtained, Table 16, show more explicitly that excepting the industrial worker group the fertility of the poorer Stockholm families was lower than that of the better situated, and that this lower fertility, observed with simultaneous analysis according to both occupation and income, was in no way a result of the greater frequency of employment of wife but was apparently a more fundamental attribute of the poorer classes in Stockholm.

To summarize: taking the reported occupation of husband in 1920 as given in the census records, a division of the

Stockholm material was made into four occupational groups. In examination of the fertility differentials subdivision of each of these four groups was made according to income of husband, age of wife, and duration of marriage. With rates standardized in respect to these last two factors, the fertility of the industrial workers was found to be highest in the group with lowest income and to decrease slightly with improved economic status. In all three of the other occupation groups, however, the reverse was observed, fertility rising unmistakably with income. Furthermore, little consistent difference in fertility was to be observed between these latter occupation groups, either in total fertility or in the fertility of the various income subgroups. No change in these relationships was produced by restriction of comparison to the fertility rates of non-employed wives.

Excepting those for the industrial workers, the observations were unusual in two respects: — first, in the general increase of fertility with income; second, in the absence of marked differences in fertility between the occupational groups. This latter may be interpreted as a result of too crude an occupational classification; it may also be attributed to the reduction of comparison to a relatively specific basis, with elimination of occupational differences in age, in marriage duration and in income.

## D.  Discussion of Observations.

In the above sections has been given a summarization of the evidence that the social class differential of intramarital fertility in Stockholm, 1919 to 1922, was the reverse of the traditional type. In so far as the statistical analysis was able to go, the existence of this uncommon type of differential fertility was well established; the original material itself was of unusual reliability and completeness. In testing the validity of the observations, therefore, the questions to be asked are: —

1) whether the sample of families included in the investigation was representative of the total childbearing population of Greater Stockholm;

2) whether the unusual fertility differentials obtained were in any way attributable to the technique of analysis employed;

3) whether there were any special conditions, either in Stockholm or in the four year study period, which may have produced the reversal of fertility relationships.

In so far as the material itself was concerned, it was absolutely representative, the only selection being in taking families in which husband and wife were living together in 1920 and in which the wife was less than forty years of age at the date of census. Within these limits, all families living in Greater Stockholm in 1920 were included in the investigation. The completeness with which the mothers of children born in 1919 to 1922 could be identified in the family records removed the possibility of non-identification as a serious source of error. The Swedish system of assigning births to place of residence of parents insured information concerning all children born to inhabitants of Stockholm. Separation of parents or change of residence in 1921 and 1922 was found to be too infrequent to affect the results. There is therefore no doubt that the observed fertility relationships did actually exist in Stockholm during the study period.

As regards statistical technique, the purpose of the study, as explained in the introductory chapter, was to make comparisons of the various social groups in terms of *specific fertility* rather than total or net reproductivity: — that is, to compare fertility under highly specific or standard conditions. The greater fertility of the upper class families shown in this chapter was demonstrated with rather specialized treatment of the statistical material, fertility being measured by the average number of live births per thousand years of married life, and with specification or standardization of marriage duration, age of parents, and employment of wives. While comparison of fertility is thereby transferred to a relatively specific basis, as desired, the results may be suspected of considerable artificiality, and the somewhat unusual fertility differentials observed may be thought to have some connection with the detail of analysis.

By way of answer to this possible objection, it may be pointed out that the unstandardized figures included in the preceding tables of standardized fertility rates also showed a distinctly higher fertility in the better situated classes. That is, the observed fertility differentials were not produced in the process of standardization. Further evidence to the same effect is given by a brief investigation made in 1928 by the Stockholm Statistical Office[1] showing a higher birth rate for this period in the wealthier sections of the city.

It has already been indicated that the years 1919 to 1922 were abnormal in several respects: they were not only in a post-war period but also had witnessed a serious economic disturbance and a considerable if temporary increase in the birth rate. For reasons previously given it does not seem probable that the economic changes during these years had an immediate effect on either the birth rate or on the social class differentials. The increased number of births in the years 1920 and 1921 may with some confidence be attributed in a large part to the numerous marriages which took place soon after the end of the war, though perhaps in part due to a previous postponement of births. It is apparent from figures given above (Tables 11, 12, 13, 15) that the greater fertility of the families in the upper social classes was most marked in the older marriages, this suggesting the occurence of a greater number of postponed births, but comparison of the fertility rates of the recent marriages, contracted in 1919 and 1920, discloses some tendency for the highest fertility rates even there to be those of the best situated classes. The material, however, provides no evidence as to whether or not there was only a temporary reversal of direction in the social class fertility differentials during the study period. Some information bearing on this point is to be had from the data analyzed in the following chapter.

Finally, there is the question of local peculiarities which may have affected the fertility differentials. In respect to nativity, Stockholm is characterized by a low birth rate, and a very considerable amount of illegitimacy. In the city

[1] »Nativiteten och dennas förändringar i olika stadsdelar i Stockholm åren 1833—1927», Statistisk Månadskrift, XXIII, 7: 4—9, July, 1928.

of Stockholm, including about 85 % of the population of Greater Stockholm, the birth (live births) per thousand inhabitants was as follows in 1919 to 1922[1]: —

|  | 1919 | 1920 | 1921 | 1922 |
|---|---|---|---|---|
| Legitimate ............. | 10,2 | 12,1 | 10,8 | 10,0 |
| Illegimate............... | 3,2 | 5,2 | 4,5 | 3,8 |
| Total | 13,4 | 17,3 | 15,3 | 13,8 |

Of the total number of live births during this period, nearly 28 % were illegitimate; the ratio of legitimate to illegitimate births was 100: 39. While it is not possible to make a social classification of illegitimate children parellelling that employed in this chapter, it may be assumed that the social differential would be considerably changed if computed in terms of total rather than intramarital fertility.

In this connection it must be recalled that the present investigation was of the fertility of marriage in Stockholm, and that the observed social class differentials were the differentials in *intramarital* fertility. Unfortunately, however, even such differentials may be affected by social class differences in sexual behavior. In the first place, the presence in a family of children born previous to the marriage may reduce the fertility of marriage. In the second place, whatever tendency there is for marriage to take place after conception will increase the apparent fertility, at least in the early years of marriage, of the social classes in which premarital conception occurs most frequently. In the following chapter, it has been possible to make fertility rate comparisons with elimination of families in which the wife was known to have had children previous to the existing marriage. According to the evidence so obtained, the influence of previous children on the fertility of marriage was too slight to affect seriously the observed fertility differentials. As regards premarital conception, it is to be questioned whether the removal from the material of births in the first nine months of the 1919 to 1922 marriages would greatly increase the comparability

[1] Figures from Statistisk Årsbok för Stockholms Stad, 1929.

5

of the fertility rates of the various social groups. In any case, it is obvious from the material presented that even with the inclusion of births occurring in the first nine months of marriage, the observed fertility of the less well situated classes in Stockholm was below that of the better situated.[1]

In brief, the social differentials found in the fertility, 1919 to 1922, of Stockholm families were the reverse of those generally observed elsewhere. As far as the material itself was concerned, it may be considered to have been highly reliable; the unusual fertility relations were not products of the statistical technique employed, being observable also in the crude fertility rates. The question is then whether the results may have been affected by any unusual circumstances during the study period, or by local peculiarities of nativity in Stockholm. The abnormal periods of business activity and depression coming between 1919 and 1922 were not believed to have had an immediate effect on either birth rates or fertility differentials, but changes in the normal fertility relationships of the different social classes may have occurred as a post-war phenomenon. Evidence as to whether or not such a temporary change took place was not obtainable from the material at hand, but may be found in the supplementary data analyzed in the following chapter. Finally, by the nature of the original information, data concerning illegitimate children were excluded; although the high illegitimacy rates in Stockholm may not have affected the intramarital fertility differentials themselves, it is probable that the social differentials obtained with use of data for legitimate births were not the same as would have been obtained on the basis of total births.

*E. Summary.*

The investigation of the fertility of marriage in Stockholm, 1919 to 1922, was based on records for more than 39,000 families meeting the following specifications: —

1) recorded in the 1920 census as living in Greater Stockholm,

---

[1] See K. A. Edin, »The birth rate changes», Eugenics Review XX, 1929: 258—266.

2) wife less than forty years of age,
3) husband and wife living together.

Within these limits, the material was not a sample but a complete set of records for the Stockholm-resident families.

The data were obtained by combining the 1920 census returns and the birth registration records for the years 1919 to 1922, inclusive, the Stockholm-resident mothers of children born in the four-year period being identified in the 1920 census records, and the nativity and census data combined. The information assembled by means of this »identification method» was of particular value for the study of social differentials in fertility, as was noted in the introductory chapter. In particular, there was complete uniformity in the sociological classification of births and of population, and the recorded social status of parents referred to the period for which the fertility rates were computed.

Intramarital fertility rates were obtained with analysis according to occupation and income of husband in 1920. All comparisons were made with specification or standardization with respect to age of husband and wife in 1920, employment or non-employment of wife in 1920, and duration of marriage.

On comparison of the fertility rates of the different income groups, fertility was found to be in direct proportion to amount of annual income, — least in the lowest income class, highest for the families with incomes in excess of 10,000 kronor per annum. That this result was not an artifact of standardization was proved by the presence of the same relation of fertility to income in the unstandardized fertility rates.

Simultaneous division according to both occupation and income demonstrated an inverse relation of fertility to income among the industrial laborers. In all other occupational groups, however, the observed rates increased with income. Excepting the groups of industrial laborers, the fertility rates at a given income level showed little consistent variation with occupation. This was perhaps a result of too little specificity in occupational classification, but

suggests that occupational differentials in fertility are attributable to associated differences in economic status.

The social differential was found to be least, on a relative
basis, in the first years of marriage, the greater fertility of
the upper classes being most evident at a longer interval
after marriage.

The evidence developed was on the whole very consistent
in demonstrating a reversal of the traditional relation of fertility to social status. As for the validity of this observation,
the original material employed was of exceptional completeness and reliability.

# CHAPTER IV.

## FERTILITY OF STOCKHOLM FAMILIES, 1917 to 1930.[1]

### A. Description of material.

THE original material treated in the preceding chapter was obtained by a combination of retrospective (census) and registration data, the two supplementing each other to give information of particular value in the study of social differentials in fertility. By this combination the inherent weaknesses of each type of source material, when used alone in the study of differential fertility, were eliminated. Entire uniformity in the social classification of total population and of parents was obtained, and the classification was made according to the social status in the years of most active childbearing, when the influence on fertility of social conditions was presumably most direct. To secure the latter, study was necessarily confined to a narrow range of years before and after the 1920 census so that the social status, however defined, might without serious error be assumed to have remained constant during the interval of study. Such a procedure, however, gave only a cross-sectional study of fertility, the fertility observations confined to a period of a few calendar years and covering marriages of varying durations. The years included being abnormal in several respects it became difficult, as was observed, to distinguish between temporary disturbances and more permanent changes in fer-

---

[1] Preliminary report of this investigation has been made in articles five and six of the list given in footnote 2 of Chapter III, these reports covering the data for the 1919 marriages only and making no analysis of the relation of educational status to fertility, but being otherwise essentially parallel to the account given below.

tility and in social differentials. A dilemma was thus presented: — either to obtain constancy of social status by restriction of study to a brief period, or to cover an adequate time interval with resultant loss of accuracy in social classification.

This apparent impasse was, however, avoidable, the solution adopted being the use of a measure of fertility which was less susceptible to temporary fluctuations. To consider the specific instance encountered above: — even though the unusual character of the years around 1920 may have produced temporary changes in the birth rate and in the social differentials of intramarital fertility, it is to be questioned whether there was any permanent change in the average size of family in Stockholm. That is, the effect, if any, of the unusual circumstances may well have been to produce temporary postponement or acceleration of births but will not necessarily have affected appreciably the average fertility of marriage, particularly in a population group where, as in Stockholm, there already existed a well established preference for the small size of family.

The obvious method to free fertility computations from the effects of occasional fluctuations was therefore to make not cross-sectional but longitudinal study, to use a measure of intramarital fertility based not on data for a short calendar interval of time but rather on family records covering a given marriage duration period, extending observation of each family considered over a sufficient period of marriage to eliminate the effects of any temporary variations in fertility.

Statistical material of the desired type was provided by the »double census» method mentioned in the introductory chapter, thus giving for selected families a combination of the information contained in two censuses, use being made in particular of the social status reported in the earlier and the nativity data contained in the later census. An account is given below of the results obtained by application of this method in a study of the fertility of marriage in Stockholm. To permit the identification of a sufficient number of families it was necessary in practice to use data of consecutive censuses. To eliminate disturbance by possible trends in fertility and to give significance to the social status recorded at the time of the first census, the study was restricted to the marriages contracted in the four-year period immediately preceding the first census date.

It is recognized that even with restriction of observation to a ten-year period, a considerable element of selection was introduced by the necessary limitation of study to those families living in Stockholm at both censuses. That is, the material obtained was selected in that all families broken up by death or separation and all families moving out of Stockholm were automatically excluded, this selection being inevitable in the »double census» method. The effect of this selection on the observed fertility differentials is not known. The disturbance produced may not have been serious, but it is hoped that investigation of this point may be made later.

In the investigation of fertility in Stockholm in 1919 to 1922, cards had been made out for each family recorded in the 1920 census as living in Greater Stockholm, exclusion being only in case the wife was born before 1881 or was separated from her husband. A considerable number of these families were re-identified in the 1930 census records, and the two sets of data combined. Analysis was confined to the information obtained for 6,629 families meeting the following specifications: —

a) marriage in the four-year period 1917 to 1920, inclusive;

b) wife less than 35 years old at marriage;

c) husband and wife living together and in Stockholm (proper) in 1920 and 1930;

d) family identified in both censuses.

A careful search was made to obtain record of all children born to these families. Four sources of information in all were examined.

1. The census returns, 1920 and 1930: listing all living children, whether residing at home or not, and all deceased children, together with date of birth of each. If the marriage was childless a definite statement to that effect was given.

2. The Stockholm birth and death registers: giving a record of all children born to residents of Stockholm in the years 1917 to 1930 inclusive, — a valuable check on the completeness of the census reports, particularly on the reporting of neo-natal deaths.[1]

3. The Stockholm family register:[2] supplementing the birth registers in case the family had moved out of the city and returned during the intercensal period. Particular note was made of all first and last births.

4. Maternity hospital records: giving a record of all previous confinements. The births reported in the family registers, birth registers or census returns were searched for in the hospital records (especially the last and first births), in order to find information concerning previous births.

All the information so obtained was compared and combined to give complete nativity data. In case of contradiction a careful search was made to establish the facts. The recorded date of marriage was checked with the birth and marriage registers, and if necessary by inquiry at the parish registration offices. Particular care was taken in determining this date since only live births occurring in the first ten years of marriage were to be included in the analysis of fertility.[3]

Classification of the original material was made according to the following factors:

1. Age of husband and wife at marriage,
2. Income of husband in 1920,
3. Education of husband as reported in 1930.
4. Employment of wife, 1920.

[1] Comparison of the birth and family register information concerning the 1919 marriages with the 1930 census reports of number of children per family showed a total of eight children included in the census records but not found in the registers, as against thirty-nine to be found only in the registration material. Of the group of eight children, three were born shortly before marriage of the parents, and the majority died shortly after birth. Of the thirty-nine lacking in the 1930 census returns, all had died before the date of census, — nineteen within three days of birth, eleven more within the first month of life.

[2] The population register, in the municipal registration office, which is arranged according to households.

[3] Thus the observation period for marriages contracted in 1917 ended in 1927, on the exact anniversary of marriage.

Supplementary divisions were also made according to total number of children per family; births in the first nine months, in the first three years, in the succeeding seven years of marriage; relation of 1920 income to 1930 income of husband; birthplace of husband and wife; presence or absence of illegitimate children. Information concerning illegitimate children was obtained from the maternity hospital records and from the Child Welfare Committee (Barnavårdsnämnden). No tabulation of the material was made according to occupation of husband, the investigation being in particular concerned with the relation of education to fertility, and the combination in analysis of educational status and income promising to be fully as informative as the combination of income and occupation.

As before, income of husband and not total family income was used in classification. Furthermore, it was necessary to use the income data for 1920, not for year of marriage, the expense involved in searching for income reports of non-census years being prohibitive. However, although income differences in 1920 did not have the same significance for the 1920 marriages as for those contracted several years earlier, it should be noted that the reported incomes were used merely to give an approximate classification according to relative economic status, not to fix average or typical income for any considerable period. For separation of the families with low, medium and high economic status, the 1920 income data were probably adequate.

From the 1930 census records[1], reports were obtained of the amount of education received by husband and wife. In classifying the Stockholm family material, however, only education of husband was used, preliminary examination having shown that the wives had seldom reported an advanced education. While the report of degree of education was made at an interval of from ten to fourteen years after marriage, in only exceptional cases was education completed after marriage.

[1] The two principal innovations in the 1930 census were addition of degree of education, and date of birth of all children including those dead before census date and those not living at home.

The classification of wives as employed or not employed was again made on the basis of reported income, the employed category corresponding to an earned income of three hundred or more kronor in 1920. It would admittedly have been desirable to have taken into account the wife's status in 1930 also, but too many subdivisions of the data had to be avoided. There was indeed the possibility of considering as employed only those wives working in both 1920 and 1930, but such a procedure would have considerably decreased the number so classified, though perhaps accentuating their relative under-fertility. In any case, employment in the early years of marriage was considered to be the significant variable. As with the income of husband, it was necessary to limit the observation of income of wife to the census year although it was apparent that the significance of employment at that time depended in some degree on the duration of marriage.

### B. Fertility and educational status: the first decade of marriage.

A four-fold classification according to educational status of husband was employed, as follows.

A. »Folkskolan» or less, the »folkskolan» including the first eight years of education, from about the seventh to the fifteenth year of age.

B. Further education than »folkskolan» but without the matriculation examination.

C. With matriculation examination, usually taken at about age 18 or 19 and required for admission to universities and to the higher civil service positions.

D. Degree from university or higher technical school.

The educational status distribution of the 6,629 Stockholm families is given in Table 17 together with the corresponding numbers of live births in the first ten years of marriage. The measure of fertility employed was the average number of live births per family in this period. Although multiplication of these averages by one hundred converts them to the base used in the preceding chapter — the average number of live births per thousand years of marriage —

**Table 17.   Average  number  of live  births  in  the  first  ten years
of marriage, 6,629 Stockholm families.**

| Age of wife at marriage | | Education of husband | | | | |
|---|---|---|---|---|---|---|
| | | A | B | C | D | Total |
| Under 25 | Families ...... | 1 824 | 546 | 91 | 190 | 2 651 |
| | Births ........ | 2 509 | 885 | 152 | 396 | 3 942 |
| | Average ...... | 1.38 | 1.62 | 1.67 | 2.08 | 1.49 |
| 25—29 | Families ...... | 1 762 | 614 | 91 | 173 | 2 640 |
| | Births ........ | 1 968 | 800 | 146 | 267 | 3 181 |
| | Average ...... | 1.12 | 1.30 | 1.60 | 1.54 | 1.20 |
| 30—34 | Families ...... | 942 | 275 | 43 | 78 | 1 338 |
| | Births ........ | 840 | 262 | 48 | 99 | 1 249 |
| | Average ...... | 0.89 | 0.95 | 1.12 | 1.27 | 0.93 |
| Total | Families ...... | 4 528 | 1 435 | 225 | 441 | 6 629 |
| | Births ........ | 5 317 | 1 947 | 346 | 762 | 8 372 |
| | Average ...... | 1.17 | 1.36 | 1.54 | 1.73 | 1.26 |

the conversion does not give strict comparability, the rates
so obtained in the present chapter being averages for a definite ten year period of marriage, while the rates of the
preceding chapter were obtained as averages for a four-year
period of observation and referred to different marriage
duration intervals.

The fertility in the group of Stockholm families was
found to be lowest with least education and to increase
regularly with further education (Table 17).   In fact, the
average fertility in the first ten years of marriage was nearly
one-half greater for families of the highest education group
than for those in the lowest group (average of 1.73 against
1.17 children). As was to be expected, the number of families at the highest education level was comparatively small
and was further reduced by the necessary subdivision according to age of wife at marriage, but the observed relation
of fertility to education was consistent in all age divisions of
the material. Degree of education being, like income, an
indirect but reliable index of social status, these observations
give further evidence that the social class fertility differentials for Stockholm families were the reverse of the
customary type.

## C. Fertility in the first three years of marriage.

To discover whether any temporary changes in fertility occurred in the immediate post-war period, a subdivision of the original material was made and the fertility rates computed separately for the first three years and for the following seven years of marriage. The rates so obtained for the two marriage duration intervals (Table 18) were expressed as before as the average number of live births per family in the given interval, not converted to a per annum basis. While the number of families in each education category remained unchanged, the corresponding numbers of births were reduced by this subdivision and the computed rates showed somewhat greater variability, but the higher fertility of the upper educational groups was apparent in both periods of marriage. That is, the relative under-fertility of the lower groups was apparently not merely a temporary or post-war phenomenon.

**Table 18. Average number of live births per family in the first three years and in the succeeding seven years of marriage, 6,629 Stockholm families.** [1]

| Marriage period | Age of wife at marriage | Education of husband | | | | |
|---|---|---|---|---|---|---|
| | | A | B | C | D | Total |
| 0—3 years | Under 25.... | 0.83 | 0.96 | 0.87 | 1.16 | 0.89 |
| | 25—29 ...... | 0.67 | 0.76 | 0.88 | 0.80 | 0.71 |
| | 30—34 ...... | 0.53 | 0.53 | 0.72 | 0.72 | 0.55 |
| | Total | 0.71 | 0.79 | 0.84 | 0.94 | 0.75 |
| 4—10 years | Under 25.... | 0.54 | 0.66 | 0.80 | 0.93 | 0.60 |
| | 25—29 ...... | 0.45 | 0.55 | 0.73 | 0.75 | 0.50 |
| | 30—34 ...... | 0.36 | 0.42 | 0.40 | 0.55 | 0.39 |
| | Total | 0.47 | 0.57 | 0.69 | 0.79 | 0.52 |

For more conclusive evidence, a further division was made separating the marriages contracted in the post-war period, 1919 to 1920, from those of the preceding two years, — this in view of the fact that the marriage duration groups employed above did not correspond to a definite group of calendar years, the figures for the first three years of mar-

[1] Original figures in Appendix, Table 10.

riage for example including births occurring from 1917 to 1923 inclusive. Average fertility rates were then computed for the two marriage groups — the war period and the post-war marriages — with continued separation of data for the first three years of marriage (Table 19). For statistical adequacy it was necessary to combine the two upper education classes, but the essential division with respect to age of wife at marriage was continued.

The relative fertilities of the three education classes were found to be essentially the same in the war period marriages as in those contracted in the immediate post-war years (1919 and 1920). Further, this general similarity existed both in the first three years of marriage and in the following seven years of the first marriage decade.

It is true that some tendency appeared for the post-war marriages to have the lower average fertility, and for the fertility differentials in the first three years of marriage to

Table 19.  Average number of live births per family according to year of marriage, marriage duration and education of husband in 6,629 Stockholm families. [1]

| Year of marriage | Marriage duration .. | 0—3 years | | | 4—10 years | | | 0—10 years | | |
|---|---|---|---|---|---|---|---|---|---|---|
| | Education group.... | A | B | C+D | A | B | C+D | A | B | C+D |
| 1917 and 1918 | Wife under 25 | 0.82 | 0.97 | 1.11 | 0.58 | 0.66 | 0.88 | 1.39 | 1.63 | 1.99 |
| | »    25—29 | 0.67 | 0.76 | 0.84 | 0.47 | 0.57 | 0.79 | 1.14 | 1.33 | 1.64 |
| | »    30—34 | 0.56 | 0.63 | 0.78 | 0.40 | 0.46 | 0.54 | 0.96 | 1.09 | 1.32 |
| | Total | 0.71 | 0.81 | 0.94 | 0.50 | 0.58 | 0.79 | 1.21 | 1.39 | 1.74 |
| 1919 and 1920 | Wife under 25 | 0.85 | 0.96 | 1.02 | 0.50 | 0.66 | 0.89 | 1.36 | 1.61 | 1.91 |
| | »    25—29 | 0.67 | 0.75 | 0.80 | 0.42 | 0.53 | 0.67 | 1.09 | 1.28 | 1.48 |
| | »    30—34 | 0.51 | 0.44 | 0.68 | 0.33 | 0.38 | 0.46 | 0.83 | 0.82 | 1.14 |
| | Total | 0.71 | 0.77 | 0.87 | 0.43 | 0.55 | 0.72 | 1.14 | 1.32 | 1.59 |

be more marked for the families formed in 1917 and 1918, but in view of the weakness of these tendencies and the statistical limitations of the data these indications could not be considered significant. Rather, the statistical evidence was that the post-war and abnormal economic conditions of the

[1] Original figures in Appendix Table 11.

period had little or no appreciable effect on the average and differential fertility of marriage in Stockholm.

It may be further noted that the greater fertility of the higher education groups was uniformly less marked in the first three years than in the following seven years of the first decade of marriage. It must be remembered, however, that live births occurring in the first nine months of marriage were included in the computation of fertility rates, and that this inclusion would tend to increase the apparent fertility in the first years of marriage of those social classes in which prenuptial conception was most frequent.

## D. Education, income and fertility of marriage.

While the unusual fertility differentials of the various education groups were apparently not produced by temporary changes occurring in the post-war period, a second possibility was that the observed relation of education of husband to the fertility of marriage actually depended on inequalities in the distribution of economic status. To check this point fertility rates were accordingly prepared with specification of both educational status and income in 1920 of husband (Table 20).

Table 20. Average number of live births per family in the first ten years of marriage, according to education and income of husband in 6,629 Stockholm families. [1]

| Income of husband (kronor) | Education group | | | |
|---|---|---|---|---|
| | A | B | C+D | Total |
| Under 4,000 ............ | 1.15 | 1.18 | 1.46 | 1.16 |
| 4—6,000 ................ | 1.18 | 1.34 | 1.45 | 1.21 |
| 6—10,000................ | 1.18 | 1.35 | 1.46 | 1.31 |
| 10,000 or over .......... | 1.56 | 1.62 | 1.85 | 1.74 |
| Under 6,000 ............ | 1.17 | 1.28 | 1.45 | 1.19 |
| 6,000 or over ............ | 1.23 | 1.45 | 1.70 | 1.47 |
| Total | 1.17 | 1.36 | 1.66 | 1.26 |

[1] Original figures in Appendix Table 12.

Well defined educational status differentials in fertility persisted after this division of the material with respect to income class of husband. At each income level the average number of children per family increased without exception from the lowest to the highest education groups. As may be seen from Appendix Table 12, the numbers in certain sections of the material become rather small in subdivision, but in view of the consistency of the evidence no standardization or statistical comparison of rates was considered necessary.

The above observations, based on the figures of Table 20, were, however, made without distinction of age of wife. In as much as the age factor had been found to affect considerably the fertility of marriage, further subdivision was made with respect to age of wife at marriage (Table 21). To obtain statistical adequacy, only two income groups were employed, under and over 6,000 kronor per annum. As a further check separate rates were also computed for the non-employed wives only in the lower income classes[1]

**Table 21. Average number of live births in the first ten years of marriage, according to education and income of husband, age and employment of wife at marriage in 6,629 Stockholm families.** [2]

| Income of husband kronor | Age of wife at marriage | Education group | | | |
|---|---|---|---|---|---|
| | | A | B | C+D | Total |
| Under 6,000 (wife non-employed) | Under 25 ...... | 1.48 | 1.64 | 1.90 [3] | 1.51 |
| | 25—29 ........ | 1.23 | 1.25 | 1.34 [3] | 1.23 |
| | 30—34 ........ | 0.99 | 1.02 | 0.91 [3] | 0.99 |
| Under 6,000 (total) | Under 25 ...... | 1.37 | 1.59 | 1.83 [3] | 1.42 |
| | 25—29 ........ | 1.11 | 1.16 | 1.33 [3] | 1.12 |
| | 30—34 ........ | 0.87 | 0.88 | 0.73 [3] | 0.87 |
| 6,000 or over (total) | Under 25 ...... | 1.42 | 1.66 | 1.97 | 1.73 |
| | 25—29 ........ | 1.19 | 1.46 | 1.61 | 1.43 |
| | 30—34 ........ | 1.04 | 1.04 | 1.28 | 1.12 |

[1] No classification according to employment and non-employment of wife was to be had for families in which the husband's income was at least 6,000 kronor in 1920.

[2] Original figures in Appendix Table 13.

[3] Rates based on observations for less than 50 families.

(Table 21). In spite of inadequate numbers in certain sections of the material, the evidence was in accord with that previously obtained: — the observed fertility of marriage increased from the lower to the higher education groups.

In brief: according to the statistical evidence so far obtained, the greater intramarital fertility of the more educated Stockholm groups was not only apparent but real, depending neither on better economic status nor on more favorable age and employment distribution of wives.

## E. Illegitimacy and the fertility of marriage.

A further possibility was that the greater amount of illegitimacy in certain sections of the Stockholm population may have reduced their intramarital fertility. It is true that the investigations reported above were not directly concerned with illegitimate births since comparison of the fertility of different social classes was made in terms of intramarital fertility only, but even this basis of comparison may have been indirectly affected by an unequal distribution of illegitimacy. That is, the observed fertility of marriage may well be expected to have been less for families which contained illegitimate children (or children of a previous marriage).

An attempt was made to eliminate this possible fallacy in direct comparison of the educational class fertility rates. As mentioned before, the records of all mothers belonging to the study group were searched for in the maternity hospital files; from these information was extracted concerning all previous reported confinements, with special note of those occurring before the existing marriage. The inadequacy of this material was apparent, there being no hospital record for wives childless during the study period and no assurance of completeness in reporting[1], but some supplementary information concerning illegitimate births was had from the Child

---

[1] However, the fact that definite record of illegitimate children or children of previous marriage was found for 1,590 of the 6,629 wives is, although no proof of completeness, at least evidence that the information was not fragmentary.

Welfare Committee (Barnavårdsnämnden). On the basis of the available information a reclassification of the entire material was made, separating the wives known to have had illegitimate children or children in previous marriages from those having no known confinements before the observed marriage period. A summary of the data for the latter group is given in Table 22. (See also Appendix C.)

**Table 22. Percentage distribution of number of live births per family in the first ten years of marriage, 5,039 Stockholm families in which the wife was not known to have had children previous to the observed marriage.**

| Income of husband kronor | Education | Total families | Births | Average per family | Number of live births | | | |
|---|---|---|---|---|---|---|---|---|
| | | | | | 0 | 1 | 2 | 3+ |
| Under 6,000 | A ...... | 2 808 | 3 332 | 1.19 | 29.1 | 37.1 | 23.7 | 10.1 |
| | B ...... | 651 | 882 | 1.35 | 23.2 | 33.9 | 29.8 | 13.1 |
| | C+D .. | 91 | 132 | 1.45 | 23.1 | 30.8 | 27.4 | 18.7 |
| | Total | 3 550 | 4 346 | 1.22 | 27.9 | 36.3 | 24.9 | 10.9 |
| 6,000 or over | A ...... | 361 | 472 | 1.31 | 25.5 | 33.8 | 28.2 | 12.5 |
| | B ...... | 595 | 888 | 1.49 | 22.5 | 27.1 | 33.3 | 17.1 |
| | C+D .. | 533 | 931 | 1.75 | 16.9 | 25.1 | 31.0 | 27.0 |
| | Total | 1 489 | 2 291 | 1.54 | 21.2 | 28.0 | 31.2 | 19.6 |
| Total | A ...... | 3 169 | 3 804 | 1.20 | 28.7 | 36.7 | 24.2 | 10.4 |
| | B ...... | 1 246 | 1 770 | 1.42 | 22.9 | 30.6 | 31.5 | 15.0 |
| | C+D .. | 624 | 1 063 | 1.70 | 17.8 | 26.0 | 30.4 | 25.8 |
| | Total | 5 039 | 6 637 | 1.32 | 25.9 | 33.9 | 26.8 | 13.4 |

In spite of rather small numbers in certain sections of the material, the higher fertility of the more educated groups was about as strongly indicated as before removal of the data for families with known premarital births. Similarly, the fertility in the higher income groups was still consistently above that of families with lower income. With regard to the previously mentioned effect of the inclusion of births occurring in the first nine months of marriage it may be noted, in section C above, that even with the inclusion of these births the observed fertility of the lower education groups was less than that of the more educated.

More detailed evidence concerning the relative fertility

of the various social divisions was given by distribution of the material according to number of live births in the first decade of marriage (Table 22). The frequency of childless and one-child marriages was found to decrease, going from the lower to the higher education divisions and from the lower to the higher income group. The large size family (three or more live births in the first decade of marriage) represented on the average from one-fourth to one-fifth of the highest income and education group cases as compared to only one-tenth in the lowest group.

Comparison of fertility rates indicated that the influence of previous births on the average fertility of marriage was relatively slight, although this influence would undoubtedly have been more apparent if account had been taken of the number of such births.[1]

While these observations must be taken with caution in view of the unknown completeness of information, the available evidence was at least uniform in indicating that social class differences in the number of premarital births were in no way responsible for the higher intramarital fertility of the more educated Stockholm groups.

To summarize: it was shown that, with classification of the Stockholm family material according to education of husband, fertility in the first decade of marriage was higher for the more educated than for the less educated classes in Stockholm. In confirmation it was demonstrated that the higher fertility of the more educated was not a temporary post-war phenomenon, that it was not merely a result of a generally more favorable economic status in the more educated classes, that it was not attributable to differences between the social classes in age distribution or frequency of employment of wives, that in all probability it was not a result of class differences in the number of children born before the observed marriages. For supplementary evidence and information, a few additional tabulations of the original material are given in the following sections.

[1] Under the circumstances, no information was to be had concerning the *de facto* marriages which were never legalized, or which were not legalized until after 1920.

*F. Fertility in relation to changes
of income.*

Combination of the 1920 and 1930 census records for
each of the 6,629 Stockholm families gave the husband's reported income both at the beginning and at
the end of the decade. In classifying the material according to economic status, the reported income of husband in
1920 only was used, this being the most direct index of
economic status in the earliest and most fertile period of
marriage. As a supplementary analysis, however, it was
of interest to observe the change of income during the ten
year period and to discover whether such changes gave evidence of affecting the fertility of marriage.

In view of the economic situation in 1920 and 1930 it
was inadvisable to make detailed classification according to
differences of income in the two census years. All that could
be attempted was to distinguish between the families with
the more favorable and those with the less favorable changes
of income. The median ratio of 1930 income to 1920 income
was obtained and used as a point of division; families whose
income ratio exceeded the median were classified as
having a »favorable» change of income, and those falling
below assigned to the »unfavorable» group. Families in
which the husband reported an income in 1920 only were
assigned to the »unfavorable» group; similarly, families
having a reported income in 1930 but not in 1920 were classified as having a »favorable» income change. The few cases
in which the income ratio equalled the median were divided
between the two groups according to the proportions observed in the total classifiable material. The doubtful cases
in all made up only about 1.3 % of the total.

In analyzing the relation of income change to the fertility of marriage, the original material was classified
with respect to the 1920 income of husband, his age
at marriage, and his educational status as reported in
1930. The relative significance of these factors, as regards
improvement of income, is indicated in Table 23. As was
to be expected the younger men in general benefited more

**Table 23. Percentage of families with »favorable» change of income between 1920 and 1930; 6,629 Stockholm families classified by 1920 income, age at marriage, and education of husband.[1]**

| Income in 1920 (kronor) | Age of husband at marriage | Education group | | | |
|---|---|---|---|---|---|
| | | A | B | C+D | Total |
| Under 6,000 | Under 30 ...... | 48.9 | 62.9 | 75.4 [2] | 51.5 |
| | 30 or over .... | 44.0 | 57.9 | 70.6 [2] | 46.9 |
| | Total | 47.2 | 61.0 | 73.7 [2] | 50.0 |
| 6—10,000 | Under 30 ...... | 36.4 | 56.2 | 76.9 | 53.7 |
| | 30 or over .... | 28.9 | 55.1 | 58.8 [2] | 45.7 |
| | Total | 32.8 | 55.8 | 69.8 | 49.9 |
| 10,000 or over | Under 30 ...... | 42.9 [2] | 41.6 [2] | 62.8 | 53.9 |
| | 30 or over .... | 28.9 [2] | 48.2 | 50.0 | 46.9 |
| | Total | 33.3 [2] | 45.7 | 55.3 | 49.7 |

[1] Original data in Appendix, Table 14.
[2] Rates based on data for less than 100 families.

**Table 24. Average number of live births in the first ten years of marriage, 6,629 Stockholm families classified according to educational status of husband and change of income, 1920—1930. [1]**

| Income in 1920 (kronor) | Age of husband at marriage | Favorable change | | | | Unfavorable change | | | |
|---|---|---|---|---|---|---|---|---|---|
| | | A | B | C+D | Total | A | B | C+D | Total |
| Under 6,000 | Under 30 .... | 1.27 | 1.45 | 1.63 [2] | 1.31 | 1.24 | 1.30 | 1.44 [2] | 1.25 |
| | 30 or over .. | 1.02 | 1.13 | 1.33 [2] | 1.05 | 0.99 | 1 02 | 0.90 [2] | 0.99 |
| | Total | 1.19 | 1.34 | 1.53 | 1.23 | 1.15 | 1.19 | 1.23 [2] | 1.16 |
| 6—10,000 | Under 30 .... | 1.20 [2] | 1.60 | 1.50 | 1.46 | 1.21 | 1.38 | 1.50 [2] | 1.30 |
| | 30 or over .. | 1.22 | 1.35 | 1.50 | 1.35 | 1.11 | 1.04 | 1.23 [2] | 1.10 |
| | Total | 1.21 | 1.47 | 1.50 | 1.41 | 1.16 | 1.20 | 1.35 | 1.20 |
| 10,000 or over | Under 30 .... | 1.78 [2] | 2.24 [2] | 2.09 | 2.11 | 1.50 [2] | 1.54 | 1.98 | 1.74 |
| | 30 or over .. | 1.15 [2] | 1.78 | 1.88 | 1.79 | 1.69 [2] | 1.21 | 1.53 | 1.44 |
| | Total | 1.41 [2] | 1.94 | 1.98 | 1.93 | 1.64 [2] | 1.34 | 1.69 | 1.55 |

[1] Original data in Appendix Tables 14 and 15.
[2] Rates based on data for fewer than 50 families.

by increase of income than the older; on a percentage basis the income increases tended to be greater for those in the lower income groups in 1920 than for those with higher income. Most marked, however, was the great advantage of the more educated over the less educated in so far as improvement of income was concerned. This observation at once suggests that the more assured economic future of the better educated may be an important factor in determining their relatively greater fertility.

In Table 24 are given the average fertility rates of the »favorable» and »unfavorable» income change groups, with further specification of 1920 income class, age of husband at marriage, and educational status. The principal observations to be made are, in brief, a generally greater fertility in the upper income groups, a uniformly higher fertility for the families with »favorable» income change, and a quite general and apparently strong increase in fertility from the lower to the upper education divisions. With allowance for the poor representation of the more educated in the lowest income class and of the least educated in the highest income class, the evidence may be considered consistent.

## G. Summary.

The immediate objectives in the analysis of the Stockholm family data, 1917 to 1930, were to demonstrate the advantages of the type of material in study of social class differences in fertility and to develop the most important aspect of the material, — to determine the relation of educational status to the fertility of marriage in Stockholm.

The principal methodological feature of the study, discussed in the introductory section of the chapter, was the use of a longitudinal measure of fertility combined with a social classification of families according to status in the early years of marriage. Although the necessary restriction of the study to the families living in Stockholm at the time of both the 1920 and the 1930 censuses did introduce an element of selection, the compensating technical advantages of the material so obtained were considerable.

In particular, the effect of measuring the average fertility over a definite marriage duration period (the first decade of marriage) rather than over a given calendar interval was presumably to eliminate the effect of whatever temporary postponement or acceleration of births may have occured in connection with economic and social disturbances during the study period. Further, the classification of families according to social status in the years of most active childbearing insured maximum directness in the observed relationships of social factors and fertility.

The material analyzed consisted of records for 6,629 Stockholm families. The data were obtained by a combination of the 1920 and the 1930 census returns for these families, supplemented by information from the Stockholm birth registers and family registers, and from maternity hospital records.

The classification with respect to economic status was based on the 1920 income of husband, the educational status classification on the husband's degree of education as reported in the 1930 census.

The observed fertility rates increased without exception from the lowest to the highest education groups. The validity of this observation was confirmed by demonstrating: —

1. that the fertility differentials were not produced by a more favorable age distribution or a less frequent employment of wives in the more educated groups;

2. that they were not merely a result of the better economic position of the more educated;

3. that they were not a product of temporary changes in fertility during the post-war years;

4. that in all probability they were not a result of social class differences in the number of children born to the wives before the observed marriages (illegitimate children plus children of former marriages).

As a further point, analysis of fertility in the first decade of marriage was made with respect to the ratio of 1930 income to 1920 income of husband. A slightly higher than average fertility was to be observed in families having the more favorable changes in income.

Evidence was also obtained to attest the validity of the social class differentials in fertility observed in the preceding chapter. The abnormal conditions of the period around 1920 were shown to have had little or no effect on the average fertility of marriage in Stockholm; the previously observed relation of fertility to economic status was found to have been no temporary phenomenon.

# CHAPTER V.

## SUMMARY.

The objective in the preparation of this report of certain investigations of differential fertility in Sweden was three-fold: — first, to present and to illustrate the potentialities of the Swedish demographic data; second, to discuss the methodological advantages of the measures of fertility and the original material used in the reported investigations; and finally, to make a critical and somewhat more detailed analysis of the evidence of a reversal in Stockholm of the traditional social differentials in fertility.

No attempt was made to give a completely detailed account of the Swedish statistical organization and official demographic data. The general form only of the organization was outlined, with details included only in so far as essential for description of the source materials and for explanation of the statistical measures of fertility employed. From the general information and the specific illustrations given, however, the excellence of the material and the opportunities for demographic study which it offers should be apparent.

In the reported investigations, comparison of the fertility of different social classes was made in terms of multi-specific fertility rates, the attempt being to find the relative fertility under equivalent conditions, with the controllable factors known to affect fertility held constant in order that the net effect on fertility of social status might be isolated. The method employed to arrive at the true relationships consisted not so much of statistical manipulations as of purposeful selection and elaboration of the original material, this procedure being very directly associated with, in fact made possible by, the organization of the Swedish demographic data.

The principal methodological problem encountered was that of obtaining entirely comparable and reliable fertility rates for the various social groups — more specifically, to obtain entire uniformity in the sociological classifications of nativity and population data. A satisfactory solution was made possible by the detail and accuracy of the original information, and by various combinations of the data to give the desired correspondence of numerator and denominator of the fertility rate fraction.

In the foregoing analyses of the material assembled, only the principal points were developed. The detailed observations were summarized at the end of each chapter. From the evidence presented, the general conclusion to be drawn was that, for the period covered, the highest intramarital fertility in Stockholm was that of the upper classes, regardless of whether these were defined in terms of occupational, economic, or educational status. In view of the reliability of the original information and the unanimity of the statistical evidence, the fact of a reversal in Stockholm of the usual social class differentials in intramarital fertility may be considered established.

From a more general viewpoint, the principal distinction of the material and methods reviewed above lay in the possibilities they offered for detailed demographic treatment of sociological variables. In the particular applications made in the preceding chapters, the significance of social factors was considered in relation to fertility only, and the potentialities of the assembled material were only partially developed by reason of the summary nature of the reports. These limitations of treatment, however, should not conceal the existing opportunity for at once much broader range and more minute detail of study. A most promising but also most difficult field for demographic study is opened by introduction of the concept of social groupings and stratifications within otherwise homogeneous population units. For adequate treatment of social factors, population data of exceptional detail and accuracy are required: in the provision of such data lies the particular scientific value of the Swedish population records, which afford an unequalled opportunity to make factual analysis of the significance and the consequences of social conditions in terms of vital and demographic phenomena.

## APPENDIX A.

*Illegitimate confinement rates in
the Mälar counties, 1930—1931.*

Although it was not possible to make an occupational classification of illegitimate births occurring in the Mälar counties during the two years 1930 and 1931, a distribution according to community group was made for these births excluded from the data of Chapter II. The computed illegitimate confinement rates are given in Table c below, and the corresponding absolute numbers in the accompanying tabulations. The community group differences in illegitimate confinement rates were found to parallel those of the legitimate rates of Table 6, Chapter II, extramarital fertility being higher in the more agricultural communities and lower in the more urban-like districts. In effect, therefore, the community group fertility differentials would be of essentially the same order, whether computed in terms of intramarital or total fertility.

Table a. Age and community group distribution of the unmarried female population, age 15 to 44, of the rural sections of the Mälar counties as given by the census of Dec. 31, 1930.

| Age | Community group | | | | |
|---|---|---|---|---|---|
| | I | II | III | IV | Total |
| 15—19 ........ | 7 956 | 8 576 | 7 366 | 6 213 | 30 111 |
| 20—24 ........ | 4 870 | 5 581 | 5 170 | 5 059 | 20 680 |
| 25—29 ........ | 2 587 | 3 210 | 2 944 | 2 651 | 11 392 |
| 30—34 ........ | 1 624 | 2 235 | 1 864 | 1 477 | 7 200 |
| 35—39 ........ | 1 306 | 1 592 | 1 275 | 1 041 | 5 214 |
| 40—44 ........ | 1 100 | 1 317 | 1 121 | 869 | 4 407 |
| Total | 19 443 | 22 511 | 19 740 | 17 310 | 79 004 |

**Table b. Age and community distribution of the reported confinements of unmarried women, age 15 to 44, in the rural sections of the Mälar counties, 1930 and 1931.**

| Age | Community group | | | | |
|---|---|---|---|---|---|
| | I | II | III | IV | Total |
| 15—19........ | 300 | 307 | 220 | 143 | 970 |
| 20—24........ | 423 | 487 | 397 | 285 | 1 592 |
| 25—29........ | 134 | 154 | 136 | 107 | 531 |
| 30—34........ | 58 | 74 | 62 | 41 | 235 |
| 35—39........ | 36 | 39 | 32 | 24 | 131 |
| 40—44........ | 7 | 9 | 1 | 7 | 24 |
| Total | 958 | 1 070 | 848 | 607 | 3 483 |

**Table c. Average number of confinements per annum per thousand unmarried women in the rural sections of the Mälar counties, 1930 and 1931.**

| Age | I | II | III | IV | Total |
|---|---|---|---|---|---|
| 15—19 ........ | 18.9 | 17.9 | 14.9 | 11.5 | 16.1 |
| 20—24 ........ | 43.4 | 43.6 | 38.4 | 28.2 | 38.5 |
| 25—29 ........ | 25.9 | 24.0 | 23.1 | 20.2 | 23.3 |
| 30—34 ........ | 17.9 | 16.6 | 16.6 | 13.9 | 16.3 |
| 35—39 ........ | 13.8 | 12.2 | 12.5 | 11.5 | 12.6 |
| 40—44 ........ | 3.2 | 3.4 | — | 4.0 | 2.7 |
| Total | 24.6 | 23.8 | 21.5 | 17.5 | 22.0 |

## APPENDIX B.

*Relative fertility of the Swedish clergy and
the most favorably situated classes in
Stockholm.*

The Swedish clergy were selected as a comparison group,
in the first place since their economic and social status were
comparable to those of the upper social classes in Stockholm,
in the second place since they for the most part live in rural
districts where the small size of family has not yet become
as customary as in the larger cities. From biographical data
for the members of the Swedish clergy, made available
through the kindness of Håkan Ohlsson, Publisher, of
Lund, was obtained record of all births in the first decade or
marriages contracted in the years 1915 to 1922 inclusive.
For comparability with the Stockholm material, all families
in which the wife was thirty-five years of age or over at
marriage were excluded.

The corresponding Stockholm material was that for families in which the husband's income was at least 6,000
kronor in 1920 and his education the matriculation examination (groups C and D of the educational status classification).

**Table d. Distribution of families of Swedish clergy and of upper
class Stockholm families according to number of children born
in the first decade of marriage.**

|  | Number of children | | | | | | Percentage distribution | | | | | Number of children | Average per family |
|---|---|---|---|---|---|---|---|---|---|---|---|---|---|
|  | 0 | 1 | 2 | 3 | 4+ | total | 0 | 1 | 2 | 3 | 4+ | | |
| Clergy .. | 63 | 42 | 88 | 101 | 130 | 424 | 14.9 | 9.9 | 20.8 | 23.8 | 30.7 | 1 103 | 2.6 |
| Stockholm | 90 | 134 | 165 | 115 | 29 | 533 | 16.9 | 25.1 | 31.0 | 21.6 | 5.4 | 931 | 1.7 |

The figures obtained are presented in Table d. Although
little difference was to be observed in the frequency of
childless marriage, a marked preference for the one and

two child family was apparent in the Stockholm material, while the larger family (four or more children) was most common among the clergy. In terms of the average number of children per family, the fertility of the sample group of clergy was about fifty per cent greater than that of the most fertile group of Stockholm families.

## APPENDIX C.

*Frequency of childlessness in the first
decade of marriage.*

In Table 22 of the text was given a distribution, in percentage form, according to the number of live births in the first decade of marriage in 5,039 Stockholm families in which the wife was not known to have given birth to children previous to the observed marriage. In the table below (Table e), which reports the incidence of childlessness in the first decade of marriage, is given a somewhat more detailed division of this material. Because of small numbers, particularly in the upper income and education groups, presentation of the corresponding figures for wives having premarital children (illegitimate children or children of previous marriages) was not warranted.

The relation of employment of wife and of age of wife at marriage to the incidence of childlessness was particularly marked (Table e). As for the social variables, a general inverse relation of amount of education to the percent of childless marriage was noted. In the lower income division (under 6,000 kronor) the fraction of childless families was quite consistently lower in education group B than in group A. The number of families belonging to the highest education group was too small to permit the computation of separate rates. In the upper income division, the lower incidence of childlessness in the highest education group was notable.

Economic status, as measured by the 1920 income of husband, however, showed little consistent relation to the fraction of childless marriages.

Table e. Frequency of childlessness in the first decade of marriage; 5,039 Stockholm families in which the wife was not known to have had children previous to the observed marriage.

| Income of husband kronor | Age of wife at marriage | Employment of wife | A total | A families childless | A % | B total | B families childless | B % | C+D total | C+D families childless | C+D % | Total total | Total families childless | Total % |
|---|---|---|---|---|---|---|---|---|---|---|---|---|---|---|
| Under 6,000 | Under 25 | Employed | 254 | 80 | 31.5 | 44 | 8 | 18.2 | 2 | 1 | — | 300 | 89 | 29.7 |
| | | Non-employed | 934 | 131 | 14.0 | 229 | 22 | 9.6 | 38 | 3 | — | 1 201 | 156 | 13.0 |
| | | Total | 1 188 | 211 | 17.8 | 273 | 30 | 11.0 | 40 | 4 | — | 1 501 | 245 | 16.3 |
| | 25—29 | Employed | 261 | 140 | 53.4 | 78 | 27 | 34.6 | 7 | 1 | — | 346 | 168 | 48.5 |
| | | Non-employed | 823 | 214 | 26.0 | 187 | 44 | 23.5 | 30 | 8 | — | 1 040 | 266 | 25.6 |
| | | Total | 1 084 | 354 | 32.7 | 265 | 71 | 26.8 | 37 | 9 | — | 1 386 | 434 | 31.3 |
| | 30—34 | Employed | 151 | 95 | 62.9 | 33 | 21 | 63.6 | 4 | 3 | — | 188 | 119 | 63.3 |
| | | Non-employed | 385 | 158 | 44.1 | 80 | 29 | 36.2 | 10 | 5 | — | 475 | 192 | 40.4 |
| | | Total | 536 | 253 | 47.2 | 113 | 50 | 44.2 | 14 | 8 | — | 663 | 311 | 46.9 |
| | Total | Employed | 666 | 315 | 47.3 | 155 | 56 | 36.1 | 13 | 5 | — | 834 | 376 | 45.1 |
| | | Non-employed | 2 142 | 503 | 23.5 | 496 | 95 | 19.2 | 78 | 16 | — | 2 716 | 614 | 22.6 |
| | | Total | 2 808 | 818 | 29.1 | 651 | 151 | 23.2 | 91 | 21 | 23.1 | 3 550 | 990 | 27.9 |
| 6,000 or over | Under 25 | Total | 121 | 16 | 13.2 | 211 | 28 | 13.3 | 229 | 22 | 9.6 | 561 | 66 | 11.8 |
| | 25—29 | » | 165 | 47 | 28.5 | 265 | 58 | 21.9 | 209 | 44 | 21.1 | 639 | 149 | 23.3 |
| | 30—34 | » | 75 | 29 | 38.7 | 119 | 48 | 40.3 | 95 | 24 | 25.3 | 289 | 101 | 34.9 |
| | Total | » | 361 | 92 | 25.5 | 595 | 134 | 22.5 | 533 | 90 | 16.9 | 1 489 | 316 | 21.2 |

# APPENDIX TABLES

**Table 1.** Age and occupational distribution of the female population and the occupational distribution of the male and total population, in the rural section of the Mälar counties, 1930.[1]

| | Agriculture | | | Other occupations | | | Total |
|---|---|---|---|---|---|---|---|
| | workers | others | total | workers | others | total | |
| **Community Group I** | | | | | | | |
| under 15 ........ | 8 066 | 11 883 | 19 949 | 3 095 | 2 736 | 5 831 | 25 780 |
| 15—19 .......... | 4 948 | 353 | 5 301 | 2 129 | 626 | 2 755 | 8 056 |
| 20—24 .......... | 3 572 | 583 | 4 155 | 1 897 | 544 | 2 441 | 6 596 |
| 25—29 .......... | 2 669 | 1 371 | 4 040 | 1 309 | 838 | 2 147 | 6 187 |
| 30—34 .......... | 2 101 | 2 140 | 4 241 | 1 110 | 929 | 2 039 | 6 280 |
| 35—39 .......... | 1 608 | 2 488 | 4 096 | 930 | 957 | 1 887 | 5 983 |
| 40—44 .......... | 1 309 | 2 560 | 3 869 | 802 | 954 | 1 756 | 5 625 |
| 45 and over ...... | 4 062 | 11 734 | 15 796 | 3 035 | 10 135 | 13 170 | 28 966 |
| Total ............ | 28 335 | 33 112 | 61 447 | 14 307 | 17 719 | 32 026 | 93 473 |
| Males .......... | 39 627 | 34 882 | 74 509 | 10 979 | 13 896 | 24 875 | 99 284 |
| Total population .. | 67 962 | 67 994 | 135 956 | 25 286 | 31 615 | 56 901 | 192 757 |
| **Community Group II** | | | | | | | |
| under 15 ........ | 6 625 | 9 726 | 16 351 | 7 170 | 4 162 | 11 332 | 27 683 |
| 15—19 .......... | 4 319 | 312 | 4 631 | 3 009 | 1 054 | 4 063 | 8 694 |
| 20—24 .......... | 3 123 | 502 | 3 625 | 2 967 | 887 | 3 854 | 7 479 |
| 25—29 .......... | 2 392 | 1 091 | 3 483 | 2 524 | 1 196 | 3 720 | 7 203 |
| 30—34 .......... | 1 833 | 1 685 | 3 518 | 2 230 | 1 406 | 3 636 | 7 154 |
| 35—39 .......... | 1 462 | 2 130 | 3 592 | 2 096 | 1 506 | 3 602 | 7 194 |
| 40—44 .......... | 1 189 | 2 137 | 3 326 | 1 787 | 1 437 | 3 224 | 6 550 |
| 45 and over ...... | 3 958 | 10 422 | 14 380 | 6 145 | 13 377 | 19 522 | 33 902 |
| Total ............ | 24 901 | 28 005 | 52 906 | 27 928 | 25 025 | 52 953 | 105 859 |
| Males .......... | 34 562 | 29 379 | 63 941 | 27 017 | 19 352 | 46 369 | 110 310 |
| Total population .. | 59 463 | 57 384 | 116 847 | 54 945 | 44 377 | 99 322 | 216 169 |
| **Community Group III** | | | | | | | |
| under 15 ........ | 3 012 | 3 834 | 6 846 | 10 891 | 4 101 | 14 992 | 21 838 |
| 15—19 .......... | 1 989 | 185 | 2 174 | 4 116 | 1 181 | 5 297 | 7 471 |
| 20—24 .......... | 1 372 | 220 | 1 592 | 4 281 | 1 055 | 5 336 | 6 928 |
| 25—29 .......... | 1 035 | 460 | 1 495 | 3 967 | 1 307 | 5 274 | 6 769 |
| 30—34 .......... | 820 | 678 | 1 498 | 3 546 | 1 514 | 5 060 | 6 558 |
| 35—39 .......... | 716 | 881 | 1 597 | 3 097 | 1 557 | 4 654 | 6 251 |
| 40—44 .......... | 605 | 874 | 1 479 | 2 703 | 1 535 | 4 238 | 5 717 |
| 45 and over ...... | 2 145 | 4 435 | 6 580 | 8 570 | 11 371 | 19 941 | 26 521 |
| Total ............ | 11 694 | 11 567 | 23 261 | 41 171 | 23 621 | 64 792 | 88 053 |
| Males .......... | 16 046 | 12 316 | 28 362 | 43 294 | 18 496 | 61 790 | 90 152 |
| Total population .. | 27 740 | 23 883 | 51 623 | 84 465 | 42 117 | 126 582 | 178 205 |

[1] Data from the census of December 31, 1930.

## Table 1 continued.

| | Agriculture | | | Other occupations | | | Total |
|---|---|---|---|---|---|---|---|
| | workers | others | total | workers | others | total | |
| *Community Group IV* | | | | | | | |
| under 15 .... | 1 064 | 865 | 1 929 | 10 527 | 4 237 | 14 764 | 16 693 |
| 15—19 ...... | 468 | 79 | 547 | 4 381 | 1 361 | 5 742 | 6 289 |
| 20—24 ...... | 315 | 90 | 405 | 4 860 | 1 275 | 6 135 | 6 540 |
| 25—29 ...... | 291 | 131 | 422 | 4 434 | 1 442 | 5 876 | 6 298 |
| 30—34 ...... | 219 | 176 | 395 | 3 893 | 1 717 | 5 610 | 6 005 |
| 35—39 ...... | 210 | 227 | 437 | 3 599 | 1 753 | 5 352 | 5 789 |
| 40—44 ...... | 199 | 231 | 430 | 3 102 | 1 741 | 4 843 | 5 273 |
| 45 and over .. | 754 | 985 | 1 739 | 8 465 | 8 879 | 17 344 | 19 084 |
| Total ........ | 3 520 | 2 784 | 6 304 | 43 261 | 22 405 | 65 666 | 71 971 |
| Males ........ | 5 063 | 3 045 | 8 108 | 43 961 | 18 264 | 62 225 | 70 333 |
| Total population ...... | 8 583 | 5 829 | 14 412 | 87 222 | 40 669 | 127 891 | 142 304 |
| *All Community Groups* | | | | | | | |
| under 15 .... | 18 767 | 26 308 | 45 075 | 31 683 | 15 236 | 46 919 | 91 994 |
| 15—19 ...... | 11 724 | 929 | 12 653 | 13 635 | 4 222 | 17 857 | 30 510 |
| 20—24 ...... | 8 382 | 1 395 | 9 777 | 14 005 | 3 761 | 17 766 | 27 543 |
| 25—29 ...... | 6 387 | 3 053 | 9 440 | 12 234 | 4 783 | 17 017 | 26 457 |
| 30—34 ...... | 4 973 | 4 679 | 9 625 | 10 779 | 5 566 | 16 345 | 25 997 |
| 35—39 ...... | 3 996 | 5 726 | 9 722 | 9 722 | 5 773 | 15 495 | 25 217 |
| 40—44 ...... | 3 302 | 5 802 | 9 104 | 8 394 | 5 667 | 14 061 | 23 165 |
| 45 and over .. | 10 919 | 27 576 | 38 495 | 26 215 | 43 762 | 69 977 | 108 472 |
| Total ........ | 68 450 | 75 468 | 143 918 | 126 667 | 88 770 | 215 437 | 359 355 |
| Males ........ | 95 298 | 79 622 | 174 920 | 125 251 | 70 008 | 195 259 | 370 179 |
| Total population ...... | 163 748 | 155 090 | 318 838 | 251 918 | 158 778 | 410 696 | 729 534 |

**Table 2. Age distribution of the married female population, rural section of the Mälar counties, according to community group and occupational distribution; 1930.** [1]

| | Agriculture | | | Other occupations | | | Total |
|---|---|---|---|---|---|---|---|
| | workers | others | total | workers | others | total | |
| **Community Group I** | | | | | | | |
| under 15 ........ | 0 | 0 | 0 | 0 | 0 | 0 | 0 |
| 15—19 .......... | 71 | 9 | 80 | 16 | 4 | 20 | 100 |
| 20—24 .......... | 890 | 393 | 1 283 | 278 | 152 | 430 | 1 713 |
| 25—29 .......... | 1 443 | 1 247 | 2 690 | 505 | 357 | 862 | 3 552 |
| 30—34 .......... | 1 420 | 2 006 | 3 426 | 589 | 517 | 1 106 | 4 532 |
| 35—39 .......... | 1 170 | 2 354 | 3 524 | 519 | 464 | 983 | 4 507 |
| 40—44 .......... | 995 | 2 397 | 3 392 | 395 | 473 | 868 | 4 260 |
| 45 and over ...... | 2 898 | 8 930 | 11 828 | 1 274 | 4 090 | 5 364 | 17 192 |
| Total ........... | 8 887 | 17 336 | 26 223 | 3 576 | 6 057 | 9 633 | 35 856 |
| **Community Group II** | | | | | | | |
| under 15 ........ | 0 | 0 | 0 | 0 | 0 | 0 | 0 |
| 15—19 .......... | 53 | 11 | 64 | 46 | 8 | 54 | 118 |
| 20—24 .......... | 691 | 314 | 1 005 | 692 | 195 | 887 | 1 892 |
| 25—29 .......... | 1 151 | 971 | 2 122 | 1 300 | 521 | 1 821 | 3 943 |
| 30—34 .......... | 1 115 | 1 552 | 2 667 | 1 416 | 721 | 2 137 | 4 804 |
| 35—39 .......... | 1 029 | 2 024 | 3 053 | 1 471 | 830 | 2 301 | 5 354 |
| 40—44 .......... | 856 | 2 004 | 2 860 | 1 252 | 783 | 2 035 | 4 895 |
| 45 and over ...... | 2 831 | 7 917 | 10 748 | 3 583 | 5 545 | 9 128 | 19 876 |
| Total ........... | 7 726 | 14 793 | 22 519 | 9 760 | 8 603 | 18 363 | 40 882 |
| **Community Group III** | | | | | | | |
| under 15 ........ | 0 | 0 | 0 | 0 | 0 | 0 | 0 |
| 15—19 .......... | 26 | 4 | 30 | 65 | 10 | 75 | 105 |
| 20—24 .......... | 292 | 127 | 419 | 1 154 | 177 | 1 331 | 1 750 |
| 25—29 .......... | 516 | 398 | 914 | 2 260 | 595 | 2 855 | 3 769 |
| 30—34 .......... | 495 | 634 | 1 129 | 2 588 | 856 | 3 444 | 4 573 |
| 35—39 .......... | 503 | 810 | 1 313 | 2 496 | 960 | 3 456 | 4 769 |
| 40—44 .......... | 435 | 814 | 1 249 | 2 131 | 941 | 3 072 | 4 321 |
| 45 and over ...... | 1 560 | 3 408 | 4 968 | 5 793 | 4 969 | 10 762 | 15 730 |
| Total ........... | 3 827 | 6 195 | 10 022 | 16 487 | 8 508 | 24 995 | 35 017 |
| **Community Group IV** | | | | | | | |
| under 15 ........ | 0 | 0 | 0 | 0 | 0 | 0 | 0 |
| 15—19 .......... | 5 | 1 | 6 | 59 | 10 | 69 | 75 |
| 20—24 .......... | 85 | 35 | 120 | 1 163 | 193 | 1 356 | 1 476 |
| 25—29 .......... | 169 | 105 | 274 | 2 606 | 720 | 3 326 | 3 600 |
| 30—34 .......... | 166 | 163 | 329 | 2 908 | 1 157 | 4 065 | 4 394 |
| 35—39 .......... | 177 | 218 | 395 | 2 918 | 1 233 | 4 151 | 4 546 |
| 40—44 .......... | 171 | 215 | 386 | 2 520 | 1 194 | 3 714 | 4 100 |
| 45 and over ...... | 600 | 791 | 1 391 | 6 097 | 4 273 | 10 370 | 11 761 |
| Total ........... | 1 373 | 1 528 | 2 901 | 18 271 | 8 780 | 27 051 | 29 952 |

[1] Data from the census of December 31, 1930.

### Table 2 continued.

| | Agriculture | | | Other occupations | | | Total |
|---|---|---|---|---|---|---|---|
| | workers | others | total | workers | others | total | |
| *All Community Groups* | | | | | | | |
| Under 15 ........ | 0 | 0 | 0 | 0 | 0 | 0 | 0 |
| 15—19 .......... | 155 | 25 | 180 | 186 | 32 | 218 | 398 |
| 20—24 .......... | 1 958 | 869 | 2 827 | 3 287 | 717 | 4 004 | 6 831 |
| 25—29 .......... | 3 279 | 2 721 | 6 000 | 6 671 | 2 193 | 8 864 | 14 864 |
| 30—34 .......... | 3 196 | 4 355 | 7 551 | 7 501 | 3 251 | 10 752 | 18 303 |
| 35—36 .......... | 2 879 | 5 406 | 8 285 | 7 404 | 3 487 | 10 891 | 19 176 |
| 40—44 .......... | 2 457 | 5 430 | 7 887 | 6 298 | 3 391 | 9 689 | 17 576 |
| 45 and over ...... | 7 889 | 21 046 | 28 935 | 16 747 | 18 877 | 35 624 | 64 559 |
| Total ............ | 21 813 | 39 852 | 61 665 | 48 094 | 31 948 | 80 042 | 141 707 |

### Table 3 a. Age distribution of the female population in the rural section of the Mälar counties expressed in percentage of the total population, with division according to Community group and occupational classification.[1]

| Age | Community Group | | | | Occupational classification | | | |
|---|---|---|---|---|---|---|---|---|
| | I | II | III | IV | Agr. workers | Agr. others | Agr. total | Other occupations |
| | (1) | (2) | (3) | (4) | (5) | (6) | (7) | (8) |
| Under 15 | 13.4 | 12.8 | 12.3 | 11.7 | 11.5 | 17.0 | 14.1 | 11.4 |
| 15—19.. | 4.2 | 4.0 | 4.2 | 4.4 | 7.2 | 0.6 | 4.0 | 4.3 |
| 20—24.. | 3.4 | 3.5 | 3.9 | 4.6 | 5.1 | 0.9 | 3.1 | 4.3 |
| 25—29.. | 3.2 | 3.3 | 3.8 | 4.4 | 3.9 | 2.0 | 3.0 | 4.1 |
| 30—34.. | 3.3 | 3.3 | 3.7 | 4.2 | 3.0 | 3.0 | 3.0 | 4.0 |
| 35—39.. | 3.1 | 3.3 | 3.5 | 4.1 | 2.4 | 3.7 | 3.0 | 3.8 |
| 40—44.. | 2.9 | 3.1 | 3.2 | 3.7 | 2.0 | 3.7 | 2.9 | 3.4 |
| 45 and over .. | 15.0 | 15.7 | 14.9 | 13.4 | 6.7 | 17.8 | 12.1 | 17.0 |
| 15—24.. | 7.6 | 7.5 | 8.1 | 9.0 | 12.3 | 1.5 | 7.0 | 8.7 |
| 15—44.. | 20.1 | 20.5 | 22.3 | 25.4 | 23.7 | 13.9 | 18.9 | 24.0 |
| Total .. | 48.5 | 49.0 | 49.5 | 50.5 | 41.8 | 48.7 | 45.2 | 52.3 |

[1] Absolute numbers in Appendix Table 1.

**Table 3 b.  Age distribution of the female population in the four community groups, expressed in per cent of the corresponding total population, according to occupational classification.[1]**

| Age | Community Group I | | | | Community Group II | | | |
|---|---|---|---|---|---|---|---|---|
| | Agr. workers | Agr. others | Agr. total | Other occupations | Agr. workers | Agr. others | Agr. total | Other occupations |
| | (1) | (2) | (3) | (4) | (5) | (6) | (7) | (8) |
| Under 15 | 11.9 | 17.5 | 14.7 | 10.2 | 11.1 | 16.9 | 14.0 | 11.4 |
| 15—19 .. | 7.3 | 0.5 | 3.9 | 4.8 | 7.3 | 0.5 | 4.0 | 4.1 |
| 20—24 .. | 5.3 | 0.9 | 3.1 | 4.3 | 5.3 | 0.9 | 3.1 | 3.9 |
| 25—29 .. | 3.9 | 2.0 | 3.0 | 3.8 | 4.0 | 1.9 | 3.0 | 3.7 |
| 30—34 .. | 3.1 | 3.1 | 3.1 | 3.6 | 3.1 | 2.9 | 3.0 | 3.7 |
| 35—39 .. | 2.4 | 3.7 | 3.0 | 3.3 | 2.5 | 3.7 | 3.1 | 3.6 |
| 40—44 .. | 1.9 | 3.8 | 2.8 | 3.1 | 2.0 | 3.7 | 2.8 | 3.2 |
| 45 and ov. | 6.0 | 17.3 | 11.6 | 23.1 | 6.7 | 18.2 | 12.3 | 19.7 |
| 15—24 .. | 12.5 | 1.4 | 7.0 | 9.1 | 12.5 | 1.4 | 7.1 | 8.0 |
| 15—44 .. | 23.8 | 14.0 | 18.9 | 22.9 | 24.1 | 13.7 | 19.0 | 22.2 |
| Total .... | 41.8 | 48.8 | 45.2 | 56.2 | 42.0 | 48.7 | 45.3 | 53.3 |

**Table 3 b continued.**

| Age | Community Group III | | | | Community Group IV | | | |
|---|---|---|---|---|---|---|---|---|
| | Agr. workers | Agr. others | Agr. total | Other occupations | Agr. workers | Agr. others | Agr. total | Other occupations |
| | (1) | (2) | (3) | (4) | (5) | (6) | (7) | (8) |
| Under 15 | 10.9 | 16.1 | 13.3 | 11.8 | 12.4 | 14.8 | 13.4 | 11.5 |
| 15—19 .. | 7.2 | 0.8 | 4.2 | 4.2 | 5.5 | 1.4 | 3.8 | 4.5 |
| 20—24 .. | 4.9 | 0.9 | 3.1 | 4.2 | 3.7 | 1.5 | 2.8 | 4.8 |
| 25—29 .. | 3.7 | 1.9 | 2.9 | 4.2 | 3.4 | 2.2 | 2.9 | 4.6 |
| 30—34 .. | 3.0 | 2.8 | 2.9 | 4.0 | 2.6 | 3.0 | 2.7 | 4.4 |
| 35—39 .. | 2.6 | 3.7 | 3.1 | 3.7 | 2.4 | 3.9 | 3.0 | 4.2 |
| 40—44 .. | 2.2 | 3.7 | 2.9 | 3.3 | 2.3 | 4.0 | 3.0 | 3.8 |
| 45 and ov. | 7.7 | 18.6 | 12.7 | 15.8 | 8.8 | 16.9 | 12.1 | 13.6 |
| 15—24 .. | 12.1 | 1.7 | 7.3 | 8.4 | 9.1 | 2.9 | 6.6 | 9.3 |
| 15—44 .. | 23.6 | 13.8 | 19.1 | 23.6 | 19.8 | 16.0 | 18.3 | 26.2 |
| Total .... | 42.2 | 48.5 | 45.1 | 51.2 | 41.1 | 47.7 | 43.7 | 51.4 |

[1] Absolute numbers in Appendix Table 1.

**Table 4 a. Percentage of married females in the Mälar counties according to age group, expressed in per cent of the corresponding female population and with division according to community group and occupational classification.[1]**

| Age | Community Group | | | | Occupational classification | | | |
|---|---|---|---|---|---|---|---|---|
| | I | II | III | IV | Agr. workers | Agr. others | Agr. total | Other occupations |
| | (1) | (2) | (3) | (4) | (5) | (6) | (7) | (8) |
| Under 15 | 0.0 | 0.0 | 0.0 | 0.0 | 0.0 | 0.0 | 0.0 | 0.0 |
| 15—19 .. | 1.2 | 1.4 | 1.4 | 1.2 | 1.3 | 2.7 | 1.4 | 1.2 |
| 20—24 .. | 26.0 | 25.3 | 25.3 | 22.6 | 23.4 | 62.3 | 28.9 | 22.5 |
| 25—29 .. | 57.4 | 54.7 | 55.7 | 57.2 | 51.3 | 89.1 | 63.6 | 52.1 |
| 30—34 .. | 72.2 | 67.2 | 69.7 | 73.2 | 64.3 | 93.1 | 78.2 | 65.8 |
| 35—39 .. | 75.3 | 74.4 | 76.3 | 78.5 | 72.0 | 94.4 | 85.2 | 70.3 |
| 40—44 .. | 75.7 | 74.7 | 75.6 | 77.8 | 74.4 | 93.6 | 86.6 | 68.9 |
| 45 and ov.[2] | 59.4 | 58.6 | 59.3 | 61.6 | 72.3 | 76.3 | 75.2 | 50.9 |
| 15—24 .. | 12.4 | 12.4 | 12.9 | 12.1 | 10.5 | 38.5 | 13.4 | 11.9 |
| 15—44 .. | 48.2 | 47.4 | 48.6 | 50.3 | 35.9 | 87.1 | 54.2 | 45.1 |
| Total .. | 38.4 | 38.6 | 39.8 | 41.6 | 31.9 | 52.8 | 42.8 | 37.2 |

[1] Absolute numbers in Appendix Tables 1 and 2.
[2] The lower percentage married in the highest age group is due to the increasing proportion of widowed and divorced.

**Table 4 b. Percentage of married females in the four community groups of the rural section of the Mälar counties, expressed in per cent of the corresponding female population, and with division according to occupational classification.[1]**

| Age | Community Group I | | | | Community Group II | | | |
|---|---|---|---|---|---|---|---|---|
| | Agr. workers | Agr. others | Agr. total | Other occupations | Agr. workers | Agr. others | Agr. total | Other occupations |
| Under 15 | 0.0 | 0.0 | 0.0 | 0.0 | 0.0 | 0.0 | 0.0 | 0.0 |
| 15—19 .. | 1.4 | 2.5 | 1.5 | 0.7 | 1.2 | 3.5 | 1.4 | 1.3 |
| 20—24 .. | 24.9 | 67.4 | 30.9 | 17.6 | 22.1 | 62.5 | 27.7 | 23.0 |
| 25—29 .. | 54.1 | 91.0 | 66.6 | 40.1 | 48.1 | 89.0 | 60.9 | 49.0 |
| 30—34 .. | 67.6 | 93.7 | 80.8 | 54.2 | 60.8 | 92.1 | 75.8 | 58.8 |
| 35—39 .. | 72.8 | 94.6 | 86.0 | 52.1 | 70.4 | 95.0 | 85.0 | 63.9 |
| 40—44 .. | 76.0 | 93.6 | 87.7 | 49.4 | 72.0 | 93.8 | 86.0 | 63.1 |
| 45 and ov. | 71.3 | 76.1 | 74.9 | 40.7 | 71.5 | 76.0 | 74.7 | 46.8 |
| 15—24 .. | 11.3 | 42.9 | 14.4 | 8.7 | 10.0 | 39.9 | 12.9 | 11.9 |
| 15—44 .. | 37.0 | 88.5 | 56.0 | 32.8 | 34.2 | 87.1 | 53.1 | 41.8 |
| Total .... | 31.4 | 52.4 | 42.7 | 30.1 | 31.0 | 52.8 | 42.6 | 34.7 |

[1] Absolute numbers in Appendix Tables 1 and 2.

## Table 4 b continued.

| Age | Community Group III | | | | Community Group IV | | | |
|---|---|---|---|---|---|---|---|---|
| | Agr. workers | Agr. others | Agr. total | Other occupations | Agr. workers | Agr. others | Agr. total | Other occupations |
| Under 15 | 0.0 | 0.0 | 0.0 | 0.0 | 0.0 | 0.0 | 0.0 | 0.0 |
| 15—19 .. | 1.3 | 2.2 | 1.4 | 1.4 | 1.1 | 1.3 | 1.1 | 1.2 |
| 20—24 .. | 21.3 | 57.7 | 26.3 | 24.9 | 27.0 | 38.9 | 29.6 | 22.1 |
| 25—29 .. | 49.9 | 86.5 | 61.1 | 54.1 | 58.1 | 80.2 | 64.9 | 56.6 |
| 30—34 .. | 60.4 | 93.5 | 75.4 | 68.1 | 75.8 | 92.6 | 83.3 | 72.5 |
| 35—39 .. | 70.3 | 91.9 | 82.2 | 74.3 | 84.3 | 96.0 | 90.4 | 77.6 |
| 40—44 .. | 71.9 | 93.1 | 84.4 | 72.5 | 85.9 | 93.1 | 89.8 | 76.7 |
| 45 and ov. | 72.7 | 76.8 | 75.5 | 54.0 | 79.6 | 80.3 | 80.0 | 59.8 |
| 15—24 .. | 9.5 | 32.3 | 11.9 | 13.2 | 11.5 | 21.3 | 13.2 | 12.0 |
| 15—44 .. | 34.7 | 84.5 | 51.4 | 47.7 | 45.4 | 78.9 | 57.3 | 49.7 |
| Total .... | 32.7 | 53.6 | 43.1 | 38.6 | 39.0 | 54.9 | 46.0 | 41.2 |

**Table 5.** Age distribution of the married women in each community and occupational group, rural section of the Mälar counties, who had confinements in 1930 and 1931.

| | Age at confinement | Agriculture | | | Others total | Total |
|---|---|---|---|---|---|---|
| | | workers | others | total | | |
| | Under 25 | 679 | 226 | 905 | 287 | 1 192 |
| | 25—29 | 633 | 484 | 1 117 | 340 | 1 457 |
| *Community* | 30—34 | 390 | 561 | 951 | 246 | 1 197 |
| *Group I* | 35—39 | 254 | 466 | 720 | 172 | 892 |
| | 40—44 | 95 | 211 | 306 | 75 | 381 |
| | Total | 2 051 | 1 948 | 3 999 | 1 120 | 5 119 |
| | Under 25 | 522 | 184 | 706 | 497 | 1 203 |
| | 25—29 | 473 | 380 | 853 | 599 | 1 452 |
| *Community* | 30—34 | 353 | 442 | 795 | 440 | 1 235 |
| *Group II* | 35—39 | 226 | 353 | 579 | 323 | 902 |
| | 40—44 | 99 | 212 | 311 | 129 | 440 |
| | Total | 1 673 | 1 571 | 3 244 | 1 988 | 5 232 |
| | Under 25 | 221 | 69 | 290 | 683 | 973 |
| | 25—29 | 217 | 137 | 354 | 807 | 1 161 |
| *Community* | 30—34 | 154 | 152 | 306 | 619 | 925 |
| *Group III* | 35—39 | 115 | 140 | 255 | 395 | 650 |
| | 40—44 | 38 | 58 | 96 | 162 | 258 |
| | Total | 745 | 556 | 1 301 | 2 666 | 3 967 |
| | Under 25 | 64 | 18 | 82 | 643 | 725 |
| | 25—29 | 72 | 29 | 101 | 839 | 940 |
| *Community* | 30—34 | 50 | 34 | 84 | 654 | 738 |
| *Group IV* | 35—39 | 40 | 37 | 77 | 400 | 477 |
| | 40—44 | 20 | 15 | 35 | 134 | 169 |
| | Total | 246 | 133 | 379 | 2 670 | 3 049 |
| | Under 25 | 1 486 | 497 | 1 983 | 2 110 | 4 093 |
| | 25—29 | 1 395 | 1 030 | 2 425 | 2 585 | 5 010 |
| *All Community* | 30—34 | 947 | 1 189 | 2 136 | 1 959 | 4 095 |
| *Groups* | 35—39 | 635 | 996 | 1 631 | 1 290 | 2 921 |
| | 40—44 | 252 | 496 | 748 | 500 | 1 248 |
| | Total | 4 715 | 4 208 | 8 923 | 8 444 | 17 367 |

**Table 6. Fertility in Stockholm, 1919 to 1922: total years of married life and number of live births, according to age of parents at the 1920 census, period of marriage and income.**

| Income kronor | Date of marriage | Age af wife | | | | Total | |
|---|---|---|---|---|---|---|---|
| | | under 30 | | 30 to 39 | | | |
| | | years | births | years | births | years | births |
| | | A. Husband under 35 | | | | | |
| Under 4,000 | 1919—20 | 4 936.5 | 1 334 | 1 380.5 | 218 | 6 317 | 1 552 |
| | 1916—18 | 6 308 | 987 | 3 404 | 437 | 9 712 | 1 424 |
| | Before 1916 | 3 052 | 300 | 6 144 | 462 | 9 196 | 762 |
| | Total | 14 296.5 | 2 621 | 10 928.5 | 1 117 | 25 225 | 3 738 |
| 4—6,000 | 1919—20 | 5 236 | 1 405 | 1 558.5 | 273 | 6 794.5 | 1 678 |
| | 1916—18 | 7 896 | 1 348 | 4 344 | 564 | 12 240 | 1 912 |
| | Before 1916 | 4 352 | 426 | 9 428 | 734 | 13 780 | 1 160 |
| | Total | 17 484 | 3 179 | 15 330.5 | 1 571 | 32 814.5 | 4 750 |
| 6—10,000 | 1919—20 | 1 710.5 | 419 | 476.5 | 88 | 2 187 | 507 |
| | 1916—18 | 2 444 | 460 | 1 464 | 248 | 3 908 | 708 |
| | Before 1916 | 1 180 | 143 | 2 940 | 308 | 4 120 | 451 |
| | Total | 5 334.5 | 1 022 | 4 880.5 | 644 | 10 215 | 1 666 |
| 10,000 or over | 1919—20 | 815 | 245 | 218 | 47 | 1 033 | 292 |
| | 1916—18 | 1 872 | 486 | 844 | 172 | 2 716 | 658 |
| | Before 1916 | 712 | 116 | 1 652 | 214 | 2 364 | 330 |
| | Total | 3 399 | 847 | 2 714 | 433 | 6 113 | 1 280 |
| Total | 1919—20 | 12 698 | 3 403 | 3 633.5 | 626 | 16 331.5 | 4 029 |
| | 1916—18 | 18 520 | 3 281 | 10 056 | 1 421 | 28 576 | 4 702 |
| | Before 1916 | 9 296 | 985 | 20 164 | 1 718 | 29 460 | 2 703 |
| | Total | 40 514 | 7 669 | 33 853.5 | 3 765 | 74 367.5 | 11 434 |
| | | B. Husband 35 or over | | | | | |
| Under 4,000 | 1919—20 | 455 | 116 | 978 | 144 | 1 433 | 260 |
| | 1916—18 | 816 | 132 | 2 228 | 239 | 3 044 | 371 |
| | Before 1916 | 872 | 98 | 14 600 | 847 | 15 472 | 945 |
| | Total | 2 143 | 346 | 17 806 | 1 230 | 19 949 | 1 576 |
| 4—6,000 | 1919—20 | 542.5 | 115 | 1 039.5 | 173 | 1 582 | 288 |
| | 1916—18 | 1 008 | 151 | 2 380 | 287 | 3 388 | 438 |
| | Before 1916 | 1 348 | 124 | 22 388 | 1 278 | 23 736 | 1 402 |
| | Total | 2 898.5 | 390 | 25 807.5 | 1 738 | 28 706 | 2 128 |
| 6—10.000 | 1919—20 | 344.5 | 106 | 426 | 74 | 770.5 | 180 |
| | 1916—18 | 632 | 133 | 1 236 | 172 | 1 868 | 305 |
| | Before 1916 | 616 | 56 | 10 572 | 665 | 11 188 | 721 |
| | Total | 1 592.5 | 295 | 12 234 | 911 | 13 826.5 | 1 206 |
| 10,000 or over | 1919—20 | 360.5 | 107 | 353 | 63 | 713.5 | 170 |
| | 1916—18 | 760 | 176 | 1 224 | 227 | 1 984 | 403 |
| | Before 1916 | 944 | 132 | 9 912 | 807 | 10 856 | 939 |
| | Total | 2 064.5 | 415 | 11 489 | 1 097 | 13 553.5 | 1 512 |
| Total | 1919—20 | 1 702.5 | 444 | 2 796.5 | 454 | 4 499 | 898 |
| | 1916—18 | 3 216 | 592 | 7 068 | 925 | 10 284 | 1 517 |
| | Before 1916 | 3 780 | 410 | 57 472 | 3 597 | 61 252 | 4 007 |
| | Total | 8 698.5 | 1 446 | 67 336.5 | 4.976 | 76 035 | 6 422 |

108

## Table 6 continued.

| Income kronor | Date of marriage | Age of wife — under 30 years | births | 30 to 39 years | births | Total years | births |
|---|---|---|---|---|---|---|---|
| | | **C. Total** | | | | | |
| Under 4,000 | 1919—20 | 5 391.5 | 1 450 | 2 358.5 | 362 | 7 750 | 1 812 |
| | 1916—18 | 7 124 | 1 119 | 5 632 | 676 | 12 756 | 1 795 |
| | Before 1916 | 3 924 | 398 | 20 744 | 1 309 | 24 668 | 1 707 |
| | Total | 16 439.5 | 2 967 | 28 734.5 | 2 347 | 45 174 | 5 314 |
| 4—6,000 | 1919—20 | 5 778.5 | 1 520 | 2 598 | 446 | 8 376.5 | 1 966 |
| | 1916—18 | 8 904 | 1 499 | 6 724 | 851 | 15 628 | 2 350 |
| | Before 1916 | 5 700 | 550 | 31 816 | 2 012 | 37 516 | 2 562 |
| | Total | 20 382.5 | 3 569 | 41 138 | 3 309 | 61 520.5 | 6 878 |
| 6—10,000 | 1919—20 | 2 055 | 525 | 902.5 | 162 | 2 957.5 | 687 |
| | 1916—18 | 3 076 | 593 | 2 700 | 420 | 5 776 | 1 013 |
| | Before 1916 | 1 796 | 199 | 13 512 | 973 | 15 308 | 1 172 |
| | Total | 6 927 | 1 317 | 17 114.5 | 1 555 | 24 041.5 | 2 872 |
| 10,000 or over | 1919—20 | 1 175.5 | 352 | 571 | 110 | 1 746.5 | 462 |
| | 1916—18 | 2 662 | 662 | 2 068 | 399 | 4 700 | 1 061 |
| | Before 1906 | 1 656 | 248 | 11 564 | 1 021 | 13 220 | 1 269 |
| | Total | 5 463.5 | 1 262 | 14 203 | 1 530 | 19 666.5 | 2 792 |
| Total | 1919—20 | 14 400.5 | 3 847 | 6 430 | 1 080 | 20 830.5 | 4 927 |
| | 1916—18 | 21 736 | 3 873 | 17 124 | 2 346 | 38 860 | 6 219 |
| | Before 1916 | 13 076 | 1 395 | 77 636 | 5 315 | 90 712 | 6 710 |
| | Total | 49 212.5 | 9 115 | 101 190 | 8 741 | 150 402.5 | 17 856 |

**Table 7. Fertility in Stockholm, 1919 to 1922: total years of married life and number of live births for families in which the wife reported earned income of less than 300 kronor in 1920 according to age of parents at the 1920 census, period of marriage and income.**

| Income kronor | Date of marriage | Age of wife | | | | Total | |
|---|---|---|---|---|---|---|---|
| | | under 30 | | 30 to 39 | | | |
| | | years | births | years | births | years | births |
| A. Husband under 35 | | | | | | | |
| Under 4,000 | 1919—20 | 3 787.5 | 1 108 | 942.5 | 176 | 4 730 | 1 284 |
| | 1916—18 | 5 192 | 888 | 2 836 | 405 | 8 028 | 1 293 |
| | Before 1916 | 2 516 | 276 | 5 000 | 417 | 7 516 | 693 |
| | Total | 11 495.5 | 2 272 | 8 778.5 | 998 | 20 274[1] | 3 270 |
| 4—6,000 | 1919—20 | 4 122.5 | 1 170 | 1 195.5 | 219 | 5 318 | 1 389 |
| | 1916—18 | 6 920 | 1 276 | 3 680 | 527 | 10 600 | 1 803 |
| | Before 1916 | 3 780 | 405 | 8 228 | 673 | 12 008 | 1 078 |
| | Total | 14 822.5 | 2 851 | 13 103.5 | 1 419 | 27 926 | 4 270 |
| 6—10,000 | 1919—20 | 1 402 | 365 | 334 | 67 | 1 736 | 432 |
| | 1916—18 | 2 252 | 444 | 1 236 | 219 | 3 488 | 663 |
| | Before 1916 | 1 116 | 136 | 2 712 | 293 | 3 828 | 429 |
| | Total | 4 770 | 945 | 4 282 | 579 | 9 052 | 1 524 |
| B. Husband 35 or over | | | | | | | |
| Under 4,000 | 1919—20 | 400 | 106 | 758 | 128 | 1 158 | 234 |
| | 1916—18 | 724 | 126 | 1 764 | 209 | 2 488 | 335 |
| | Before 1916 | 764 | 95 | 12 320 | 788 | 13 084 | 883 |
| | Total | 1 888 | 327 | 14 842 | 1 125 | 16 730 | 1 452 |
| 4—6,000 | 1919—20 | 449.5 | 104 | 758.5 | 151 | 1 208 | 255 |
| | 1916—18 | 920 | 146 | 1 968 | 266 | 2 888 | 412 |
| | Before 1916 | 1 212 | 120 | 19 396 | 1 205 | 20 608 | 1 325 |
| | Total | 2 581.5 | 370 | 22 122.5 | 1 622 | 24 704 | 1 992 |
| 6—10,000 | 1919—20 | 293 | 92 | 337 | 60 | 630 | 152 |
| | 1916—16 | 608 | 131 | 1 088 | 162 | 1 696 | 293 |
| | Before 1916 | 588 | 56 | 9 808 | 630 | 10 396 | 686 |
| | Total | 1 489 | 279 | 11 233 | 852 | 12 722 | 1 131 |

[1] A small group contributing only eight marriage years could not be classified according to employment of wife and has been omitted from this table. Otherwise than this, the fertility data for working wives may be obtained by subtracting the figures of Table 7 from those of Table 6.

By reason of the rarity of employment of wife in the highest income group (10,000 or over), comparable figures for that group may be obtained directly from Appendix Table 6.

Table 8. Fertility in Stockholm, 1919 to 1922: total years of married life and number of live births, with division according to age of wife at the 1920 census, period of marriage, occupation and income of husband in 1920.

| Income kronor | Date of marriage | Age of wife under 30 years | births | 30 to 39 years | births | Total years | births |
|---|---|---|---|---|---|---|---|
| A | | A. Industrial workers | | | | | |
| Under 4,000 | 1919—20 | 2 454 | 678 | 1 210 | 202 | 3 664 | 880 |
| | 1916—18 | 3 508 | 529 | 2 860 | 356 | 6 368 | 885 |
| | Before 1916 | 2 156 | 216 | 11 740 | 752 | 13 896 | 968 |
| | Total | 8 118 | 1 423 | 15 810 | 1 310 | 23 928 | 2 733 |
| 4—6,000 | 1919—20 | 2 090 | 536 | 1 047 | 191 | 3 137 | 727 |
| | 1916—18 | 3 588 | 566 | 2 860 | 332 | 6 448 | 898 |
| | Before 1916 | 2 664 | 226 | 15 172 | 975 | 17 836 | 1 201 |
| | Total | 8 342 | 1 328 | 19 079 | 1 498 | 27 421 | 2 826 |
| 6—10,000 | 1919—20 | 226.5 | 56 | 104.5 | 17 | 331 | 73 |
| | 1916—18 | 368 | 53 | 316 | 37 | 684 | 90 |
| | Before 1916 | 396 | 33 | 2 300 | 148 | 2 696 | 181 |
| | Total | 990.5 | 142 | 2 720.5 | 202 | 3 711 | 344 |
| 10,000 or over | 1919—20 | 6 | 1 | 9.5 | 1 | 15.5 | 2 |
| | 1916—18 | 8 | 2 | — | — | 8 | 2 |
| | Before 1916 | 4 | — | 56 | 4 | 60 | 4 |
| | Total | 18 | 3 | 65.5 | 5 | 83.5 | 8 |
| Total | 1919—20 | 4 776.5 | 1 271 | 2 371 | 411 | 7 147.5 | 1 682 |
| | 1916—18 | 7 472 | 1 150 | 6 036 | 725 | 13 508 | 1 875 |
| | Before 1916 | 5 220 | 475 | 29 268 | 1 879 | 34 488 | 2 354 |
| | Total | 17 468.5 | 2 896 | 37 675 | 3 015 | 55 143.5 | 5 911 |
| B | | B. Industry — Others | | | | | |
| Under 4,000 | 1919—20 | 474 | 106 | 286.5 | 38 | 760.5 | 144 |
| | 1916—18 | 656 | 115 | 536 | 64 | 1 192 | 179 |
| | Before 1916 | 424 | 48 | 2 144 | 117 | 2 568 | 165 |
| | Total | 1 554 | 269 | 2 966.5 | 219 | 4 520.5 | 488 |
| 4—6,000 | 1919—20 | 548.5 | 145 | 272 | 46 | 820.5 | 191 |
| | 1916—18 | 932 | 169 | 644 | 94 | 1 576 | 263 |
| | Before 1916 | 508 | 58 | 2 684 | 179 | 3 192 | 237 |
| | Total | 1 988.5 | 372 | 3 600 | 319 | 5 588.5 | 691 |
| 6—10.000 | 1919—20 | 447 | 100 | 217.5 | 39 | 664.5 | 139 |
| | 1916—18 | 704 | 143 | 592 | 89 | 1 296 | 232 |
| | Before 1916 | 432 | 55 | 3 052 | 225 | 3 484 | 280 |
| | Total | 1 583 | 298 | 3 861.5 | 353 | 5 444.5 | 651 |
| 10,000 or over | 1919—20 | 214 | 69 | 127 | 21 | 341 | 90 |
| | 1916—18 | 604 | 151 | 412 | 72 | 1 016 | 223 |
| | Before 1916 | 340 | 42 | 2 752 | 254 | 3 092 | 296 |
| | Total | 1 158 | 262 | 3 291 | 347 | 4 449 | 609 |
| Total | 1919—20 | 1 683.5 | 420 | 903 | 144 | 2 586.5 | 564 |
| | 1916—18 | 2 896 | 578 | 2 184 | 319 | 5 080 | 897 |
| | Before 1916 | 1 704 | 203 | 10 632 | 775 | 12 336 | 978 |
| | Total | 6 283.5 | 1 201 | 13 719 | 1 238 | 20 002.5 | 2 439 |

## Table 8 continued.

| Income kronor | Date of marriage | Age of wife | | | | Total | |
|---|---|---|---|---|---|---|---|
| | | under 30 | | 30 to 39 | | | |
| | | years | births | years | births | years | births |
| | | **C. Trade and commerce** | | | | | |
| Under 4,000 | 1919—20 | 1 462 | 381 | 560 | 95 | 2 022 | 476 |
| | 1916—18 | 1 928 | 297 | 1 544 | 171 | 3 472 | 468 |
| | Before 1916 | 908 | 95 | 4 968 | 321 | 5 876 | 416 |
| | Total | 4 298 | 773 | 7 072 | 587 | 11 370 | 1 360 |
| 4—6,000 | 1919—20 | 1 464.5 | 382 | 679 | 112 | 2 143.5 | 494 |
| | 1916—18 | 2 108 | 379 | 1 624 | 220 | 3 732 | 599 |
| | Before 1916 | 1 208 | 132 | 6 788 | 424 | 7 996 | 556 |
| | Total | 4 780.5 | 893 | 9 091 | 756 | 13 871.5 | 1 649 |
| 6—10.000 | 1919—20 | 817 | 218 | 260.5 | 50 | 1 077.5 | 268 |
| | 1916—18 | 1 252 | 235 | 996 | 169 | 2 248 | 404 |
| | Before 1916 | 448 | 56 | 3 788 | 295 | 4 236 | 351 |
| | Total | 2 517 | 509 | 5 044.5 | 514 | 7 561.5 | 1 023 |
| 10,000 or over | 1919—20 | 503 | 149 | 261 | 54 | 764 | 203 |
| | 1916—18 | 1 156 | 295 | 900 | 180 | 2 056 | 475 |
| | Before 1916 | 736 | 121 | 4 384 | 369 | 5 120 | 490 |
| | Total | 2 395 | 565 | 5 545 | 603 | 7 940 | 1 168 |
| Total | 1919—20 | 4 246.5 | 1 130 | 1 760.5 | 311 | 6 007 | 1 441 |
| | 1916—18 | 6 444 | 1 206 | 5 064 | 740 | 11 508 | 1 946 |
| | Before 1916 | 3 300 | 404 | 19 928 | 1 409 | 23 228 | 1 813 |
| | Total | 13 990.5 | 2 740 | 26 752.5 | 2 460 | 40 743 | 5 200 |
| | | **D. Arts and professions** | | | | | |
| Under 4,000 | 1919—20 | 1 001.5 | 285 | 302 | 27 | 1 303.5 | 312 |
| | 1916—18 | 1 032 | 178 | 692 | 85 | 1 724 | 263 |
| | Before 1916 | 436 | 39 | 1 892 | 119 | 2 328 | 158 |
| | Total | 2 469.5 | 502 | 2 886 | 231 | 5 355.5 | 733 |
| 4—6,000 | 1919—20 | 1 675.5 | 457 | 600 | 97 | 2 275.5 | 554 |
| | 1916—18 | 2 276 | 385 | 1 596 | 205 | 3 872 | 590 |
| | Before 1916 | 1 320 | 134 | 7 172 | 434 | 8 492 | 568 |
| | Total | 5 271.5 | 976 | 9 368 | 736 | 14 639.5 | 1 712 |
| 6—10,000 | 1919—20 | 564.5 | 151 | 320 | 56 | 884.5 | 207 |
| | 1916—18 | 752 | 162 | 796 | 125 | 1 548 | 287 |
| | Before 1916 | 520 | 55 | 4 372 | 305 | 4 892 | 360 |
| | Total | 1 836.5 | 368 | 5 488 | 486 | 7 324.5 | 854 |
| 10,000 or over | 1919—20 | 452.5 | 133 | 173.5 | 34 | 626 | 167 |
| | 1916—18 | 864 | 214 | 756 | 147 | 1 620 | 361 |
| | Before 1916 | 576 | 85 | 4 372 | 394 | 4 948 | 479 |
| | Total | 1 892.5 | 432 | 5 301.5 | 575 | 7 194 | 1 007 |
| Total | 1919—20 | 3 694 | 1 026 | 1 395.5 | 213 | 5 089.5 | 1 239 |
| | 1916—18 | 4 924 | 939 | 3 840 | 562 | 8 764 | 1 501 |
| | Before 1916 | 2 852 | 313 | 17 808 | 1 252 | 20 660 | 1 565 |
| | Total | 11 470 | 2 278 | 23 043.5 | 2 027 | 34 513.5 | 4 305 |

**Table 9.** Fertility in Stockholm, 1919 to 1922: total years of married life and number of live births for families in which the wife reported earned income of less than 300 kronor in 1920, with division according to age of wife at the 1920 census, period of marriage, and income and occupation of husband in 1920.

| Income kronor | Date of marriage | Age of wife | | | | Total | |
|---|---|---|---|---|---|---|---|
| | | under 30 | | 30 to 39 | | | |
| | | years | births | years | births | years | births |
| | | A. Industrial workers | | | | | |
| Under 4,000 | 1919—20 | 1 905 | 573 | 882.5 | 173 | 2 787.5 | 746 |
| | 1916—18 | 2 852 | 478 | 2 260 | 324 | 5 112 | 802 |
| | Before 1916 | 1 724 | 200 | 9 488 | 690 | 11 212 | 890 |
| | Total | 6 481 | 1 251 | 12 630.5 | 1 187 | 19 111.5 | 2 438 |
| 4—6,000 | 1919—20 | 1 566 | 428 | 760.5 | 158 | 2 326.5 | 586 |
| | 1916—18 | 3 064 | 530 | 2 344 | 305 | 5 408 | 835 |
| | Before 1916 | 2 280 | 212 | 12 764 | 910 | 15 044 | 1 122 |
| | Total | 6 910 | 1 170 | 15 868.5 | 1 373 | 22 778.5 | 2 543 |
| 6,000 or over | 1919—20 | 213.5 | 54 | 97 | 17 | 310.5 | 71 |
| | 1916—18 | 332 | 53 | 296 | 36 | 628 | 89 |
| | Before 1916 | 364 | 32 | 2 120 | 145 | 2 484 | 177 |
| | Total | 909.5 | 139 | 2 513 | 198 | 3 422.5 | 337 |
| Total | 1919—20 | 3 684.5 | 1 055 | 1 740 | 348 | 5 424.5 | 1 403 |
| | 1916—18 | 6 248 | 1 061 | 4 900 | 665 | 11 148 | 1 726 |
| | Before 1916 | 4 368 | 444 | 24 372 | 1 745 | 28 740 | 2 189 |
| | Total | 14 300.5 | 2 560 | 31 012 | 2 758 | 45 312.5 | 5 318 |
| | | B. Industry — Others | | | | | |
| Under 4,000 | 1919—20 | 398 | 87 | 204.5 | 32 | 602.5 | 119 |
| | 1816—18 | 560 | 107 | 456 | 60 | 1 016 | 167 |
| | Before 1916 | 396 | 48 | 1 912 | 108 | 2 308 | 156 |
| | Total | 1 354 | 242 | 2 572.5 | 200 | 3 926.5 | 442 |
| 4—6,000 | 1919—20 | 452.5 | 124 | 199.5 | 36 | 652 | 160 |
| | 1916—18 | 832 | 162 | 540 | 83 | 1 372 | 245 |
| | Before 1916 | 464 | 56 | 2 428 | 163 | 2 892 | 219 |
| | Total | 1 748.5 | 342 | 3 167.5 | 282 | 4 916 | 624 |
| 6,000 or over | 1919—20 | 583.5 | 155 | 284.5 | 50 | 868 | 205 |
| | 1916—18 | 1 256 | 288 | 876 | 151 | 2 132 | 439 |
| | Before 1916 | 740 | 95 | 5 576 | 469 | 6 316 | 564 |
| | Total | 2 579.5 | 538 | 6 736.5 | 670 | 9 316 | 1 208 |
| Total | 1919—20 | 1 434 | 366 | 688.5 | 118 | 2 122.5 | 484 |
| | 1916—18 | 2 648 | 557 | 1 872 | 294 | 4 520 | 851 |
| | Before 1916 | 1 600 | 199 | 9 916 | 740 | 11 516 | 939 |
| | Total | 5 682 | 1 122 | 12 476.5 | 1 152 | 18 158.5 | 2 274 |

## Table 9 continued.

| Income kronor | Date of marriage | Age of wife | | | | Total | |
|---|---|---|---|---|---|---|---|
| | | under 30 | | 30 to 39 | | | |
| | | years | births | years | births | years | births |
| **C. Trade and commerce** | | | | | | | |
| Under 4,000 | 1919—20 | 1 118.5 | 320 | 411 | 80 | 1 529.5 | 400 |
| | 1916—18 | 1 620 | 268 | 1 308 | 154 | 2 928 | 422 |
| | Before 1916 | 780 | 88 | 4 308 | 298 | 5 088 | 386 |
| | Total | 3 518.5 | 676 | 6 027 | 532 | 9 545.5 | 1 208 |
| 4—6,000 | 1919—20 | 1 199.5 | 322 | 526 | 92 | 1 725.5 | 414 |
| | 1916—18 | 1 916 | 366 | 1 416 | 212 | 3 332 | 578 |
| | Before 1916 | 1 072 | 127 | 6 104 | 407 | 7 176 | 534 |
| | Total | 4187.5 | 815 | 8 046 | 711 | 12 233.5 | 1 526 |
| 6,000 or over | 1919—20 | 1 146 | 331 | 437.5 | 91 | 1 583.5 | 422 |
| | 1916—18 | 2 320 | 525 | 1 772 | 339 | 4 092 | 864 |
| | Before 1916 | 1 156 | 172 | 7 796 | 648 | 8 952 | 820 |
| | Total | 4 622 | 1 028 | 10 005.5 | 1 078 | 14 627.5 | 2 106 |
| Total | 1919—20 | 3 464 | 973 | 1 374.5 | 263 | 4 838.5 | 1 236 |
| | 1916—18 | 5 856 | 1 159 | 4 496 | 705 | 10 352 | 1 864 |
| | Before 1916 | 3 008 | 387 | 18 208 | 1 353 | 21 216 | 1 740 |
| | Total | 12 328 | 2 519 | 24 078.5 | 2 321 | 36 406.5 | 4 840 |
| **D. Arts and professions** | | | | | | | |
| Under 4,000 | 1919—20 | 764 | 234 | 202.5 | 19 | 966.5 | 253 |
| | 1916—18 | 884 | 161 | 576 | 76 | 1 460 | 237 |
| | Before 1916 | 380 | 35 | 1 620 | 109 | 2 000 | 144 |
| | Total | 2 028 | 430 | 2 398.5 | 204 | 4 426.5 | 634 |
| 4—6,000 | 1919—20 | 1 354 | 400 | 468 | 84 | 1 822 | 484 |
| | 1916—18 | 2 028 | 364 | 1 348 | 193 | 3 376 | 557 |
| | Before 1916 | 1 176 | 130 | 6 328 | 398 | 7 504 | 528 |
| | Total | 4 558 | 894 | 8 144 | 675 | 12 702 | 1 569 |
| 6,000 or over | 1919—20 | 822.5 | 241 | 353 | 69 | 1 175.5 | 310 |
| | 1916—18 | 1 520 | 361 | 1 352 | 239 | 2 872 | 600 |
| | Before 1916 | 1 072 | 139 | 7 960 | 636 | 9 032 | 775 |
| | Total | 3 414.5 | 741 | 9 665 | 944 | 13 079.5 | 1 685 |
| Total | 1919—20 | 2 940.5 | 875 | 1 023.5 | 172 | 3 964 | 1 047 |
| | 1916—18 | 4 432 | 886 | 3 276 | 508 | 7 708 | 1 394 |
| | Before 1916 | 2 628 | 304 | 15 908 | 1 143 | 18 536 | 1 447 |
| | Total | 10 000.5 | 2 065 | 20 207.5 | 1 823 | 30 208 | 3 888 |

**Table 10. Number of live births in the first three years and in the following seven years of marriage, 6,629 Stockholm families. [1]**

| Age of wife at marriage | 0—3 years | | | | | 4—10 years | | | | |
|---|---|---|---|---|---|---|---|---|---|---|
| | A | B | C | D | Total | A | B | C | D | Total |
| Under 25.... | 1 523 | 525 | 79 | 220 | 2 347 | 986 | 360 | 73 | 176 | 1 595 |
| 25—29 ...... | 1 181 | 464 | 80 | 138 | 1 863 | 787 | 336 | 66 | 129 | 1 318 |
| 30—34 ...... | 499 | 147 | 31 | 56 | 753 | 341 | 115 | 17 | 43 | 516 |
| Total | 3 203 | 1 136 | 190 | 414 | 4 943 | 2 114 | 811 | 156 | 348 | 3 429 |

[1] Distribution of families and of births in Table 17 of text.

**Table 11. Number of live births in the first three years and in the following seven years of marriage in 6,629 Stockholm families; distribution of births and families according to age of wife at marriage and period of marriage.**

| Age of wife at marriage | Education group | Number of families | Number of births during marriage period | | |
|---|---|---|---|---|---|
| | | | 0—3 years | 4—10 years | Total |
| Marriages contracted during years 1917 and 1918 | | | | | |
| Under 25 | A | 917 | 751 | 528 | 1 279 |
| | B | 264 | 255 | 175 | 430 |
| | C+D | 135 | 150 | 119 | 269 |
| 25—29 | A | 874 | 584 | 413 | 997 |
| | B | 313 | 238 | 177 | 415 |
| | C+D | 141 | 119 | 112 | 231 |
| 30—34 | A | 457 | 254 | 183 | 437 |
| | B | 135 | 85 | 62 | 147 |
| | C+D | 50 | 39 | 27 | 66 |
| Total | A | 2 248 | 1 589 | 1 124 | 2 713 |
| | B | 712 | 578 | 414 | 992 |
| | C+D | 326 | 308 | 258 | 566 |
| Marriages contracted during years 1919 and 1920 | | | | | |
| Under 25 | A | 907 | 772 | 458 | 1 230 |
| | B | 282 | 270 | 185 | 455 |
| | C+D | 146 | 149 | 130 | 279 |
| 25—29 | A | 888 | 597 | 374 | 971 |
| | B | 301 | 226 | 159 | 385 |
| | C+D | 123 | 99 | 83 | 182 |
| 30—34 | A | 485 | 245 | 158 | 403 |
| | B | 140 | 62 | 53 | 115 |
| | C+D | 71 | 48 | 33 | 81 |
| Total | A | 2 280 | 1 614 | 990 | 2 604 |
| | B | 723 | 558 | 397 | 955 |
| | C+D | 340 | 296 | 246 | 542 |

Table 12. Distribution of 6,629 Stockholm families and of the births in the first ten years of marriage according to income and education of husband.

| Income of husband kronor | Group A families | Group A births | Group B families | Group B births | Group C+D families | Group C+D births | Total families | Total births |
|---|---|---|---|---|---|---|---|---|
| Under 4,000 .... | 1 799 | 2 071 | 295 | 349 | 46 | 67 | 2 140 | 2 487 |
| 4—6,000 ........ | 2 270 | 2 681 | 494 | 663 | 53 | 77 | 2 817 | 3 421 |
| 6—10,000 ...... | 393 | 462 | 416 | 563 | 215 | 313 | 1 024 | 1 338 |
| 10,000 or over .. | 66 | 103 | 230 | 372 | 352 | 651 | 648 | 1 126 |
| Under 6,000 .... | 4 069 | 4 752 | 789 | 1 012 | 99 | 144 | 4 957 | 5 908 |
| 6.000 or over.... | 459 | 565 | 646 | 935 | 567 | 964 | 1 672 | 2 464 |
| Total | 4 528 | 5 317 | 1 435 | 1 947 | 666 | 1 108 | 6 629 | 8 372 |

Table 13. Number of live births in the first decade of marriage, and distribution of 6,629 Stockholm families according to education and income of husband, age and employment of wife at marriage.

| Income of husband kronor | Age of wife at marriage | Group A families | Group A births | Group B families | Group B births | Group C+D families | Group C+D births | Total families | Total births |
|---|---|---|---|---|---|---|---|---|---|
| Under 6,000 (wife non-employed) | Under 25 | 1 322 | 1 950 | 272 | 446 | 40 | 76 | 1 634 | 2 472 |
| | 25—29 | 1 217 | 1 491 | 236 | 296 | 35 | 47 | 1 488 | 1 834 |
| | 30—34 | 619 | 610 | 104 | 106 | 11 | 10 | 734 | 726 |
| Under 6,000 (total) | Under 25 | 1 678 | 2 302 | 320 | 509 | 42 | 77 | 2 040 | 2 888 |
| | 25—29 | 1 551 | 1 716 | 325 | 377 | 42 | 56 | 1 918 | 2 149 |
| | 30—34 | 840 | 734 | 144 | 126 | 15 | 11 | 999 | 871 |
| 6,000 or over (total) | Under 25 | 146 | 207 | 226 | 376 | 239 | 471 | 611 | 1 054 |
| | 25—29 | 211 | 252 | 289 | 423 | 222 | 357 | 722 | 1 032 |
| | 30—34 | 102 | 106 | 131 | 136 | 106 | 136 | 339 | 378 |

Table 14. Classification of 6,629 Stockholm families according to education of husband, age of husband at marriage, »favorable» and »unfavorable» change of income, 1920—1930.

| Income in 1920 kronor | Age at marriage / Education group | Under 30 | | | | 30 or over | | | | Total | | | |
|---|---|---|---|---|---|---|---|---|---|---|---|---|---|
| | | A | B | C+D | Total | A | B | C+D | Total | A | B | C+D | Total |
| Under 6,000 | Favorable | 1 325 | 314 | 49 | 1 688 | 597 | 168 | 24 | 789 | 1 922 | 482 | 73 | 2 477 |
| | Unfavorable | 1 387 | 185 | 16 | 1 588 | 760 | 122 | 10 | 892 | 2 147 | 307 | 26 | 2 480 |
| | Total | 2 712 | 499 | 65 | 3 276 | 1 357 | 290 | 34 | 1 681 | 4 069 | 789 | 99 | 4 957 |
| 6—10,000 | Favorable | 75 | 113 | 100 | 288 | 54 | 119 | 50 | 223 | 129 | 232 | 150 | 511 |
| | Unfavorable | 131 | 87 | 30 | 248 | 133 | 97 | 35 | 265 | 264 | 184 | 65 | 513 |
| | Total | 206 | 200 | 130 | 536 | 187 | 216 | 85 | 488 | 393 | 416 | 215 | 1 024 |
| 10,000 or over | Favorable | 9 | 37 | 93 | 139 | 13 | 68 | 102 | 183 | 22 | 105 | 195 | 322 |
| | Unfavorable | 12 | 52 | 55 | 119 | 32 | 73 | 102 | 207 | 44 | 125 | 157 | 326 |
| | Total | 21 | 89 | 148 | 258 | 45 | 141 | 204 | 390 | 66 | 230 | 352 | 648 |

Table 15. Number of live births in the first decade of marriage classified according to education of husband, age of husband at marriage, »favorable» and »unfavorable» change of income, 1920—1930.

| Income in 1920 kronor | Age at marriage / Education group | Under 30 | | | | 30 or over | | | | Total | | | |
|---|---|---|---|---|---|---|---|---|---|---|---|---|---|
| | | A | B | C+D | Total | A | B | C+D | Total | A | B | C+D | Total |
| Under 6,000 | Favorable | 1 677 | 456 | 80 | 2 213 | 608 | 190 | 32 | 830 | 2 285 | 646 | 112 | 3 043 |
| | Unfavorable | 1 718 | 241 | 23 | 1 982 | 749 | 125 | 9 | 883 | 2 467 | 366 | 32 | 2 865 |
| | Total | 3 395 | 697 | 103 | 4 195 | 1 357 | 315 | 41 | 1 713 | 4 752 | 1 012 | 144 | 5 908 |
| 6—10,000 | Favorable | 90 | 181 | 150 | 421 | 66 | 161 | 75 | 302 | 156 | 342 | 225 | 723 |
| | Unfavorable | 158 | 120 | 45 | 323 | 148 | 101 | 43 | 292 | 306 | 221 | 88 | 615 |
| | Total | 248 | 301 | 195 | 744 | 214 | 262 | 118 | 594 | 462 | 563 | 313 | 1 338 |
| 10,000 or over | Favorable | 16 | 83 | 194 | 293 | 15 | 121 | 192 | 328 | 31 | 204 | 386 | 621 |
| | Unfavorable | 18 | 80 | 109 | 207 | 54 | 88 | 156 | 298 | 72 | 168 | 265 | 505 |
| | Total | 34 | 163 | 303 | 500 | 69 | 209 | 348 | 626 | 103 | 372 | 651 | 1 126 |